EDITED BY FRANCES EVANS
DESIGNED BY DERRIAN BRADDER
COVER DESIGN BY ANGIE ALLISON
CONSULTANCY BY JOE FULLMAN
WITH SPECIAL THANKS TO HELEN CUMBERBATCH AND CHRISTINA WEBB

FOR JESSICA, MY ALL-TIME FAVOURITE HISTORIAN — MB
FOR JAKEY B, MY ADORABLE NUISANCE — JB

First published in Great Britain in 2021 by Buster Books,
an imprint of Michael O'Mara Books Limited,
9 Lion Yard, Tremadoc Road, London SW4 7NQ

W www.mombooks.com/buster
F Buster Books
T @BusterBooks
I @buster_books

Text and layout © Mike Barfield 2021

Illustrations copyright © Buster Books 2021

A CIP catalogue record for this book is available from the British Library.

ISBN: 978-1-78055-713-7

7 9 10 8

This book was printed in October 2023 by
Shenzhen Wing King Tong Paper Products Co. Ltd.,
Shenzhen, Guangdong, China.

A DAY IN THE LIFE
OF A **CAVEMAN**, A **QUEEN**
AND **EVERYTHING IN BETWEEN**

WRITTEN BY **MIKE BARFIELD**
ILLUSTRATED BY **JESS BRADLEY**

BUSTER BOOKS

CONTENTS

WHERE IN THE WORLD?   6

INTRODUCTION   8

ANCIENT HISTORY   9

Homo erectus   10
Neanderthal   11
Caveman   12
Fantastic Beasts   13
Woolly Mammoth   14
Newsflash   16
Farmer   17

Wheel   18
Standing Stone   19
Indus Bacterium   20
Micronesian Bird   21
Egyptian Pharaoh   22
The Write Stuff   23
Egyptian Cat   24
Newsflash   26
Llama   27
Olmec Head   28
Mumun Jar   29
Greek Vase   30
Star Statues   31

Ancient Olympian   32
Historian   33
Mask Maker   34
Greek Philosopher   36
Newsflash   37
Chinese Emperor   38
Feat of Clay   39
Dye Whelk   40
War Elephant   41
Gladiator   42
Fight School   43
House in Pompeii   44
Silk-Road Camel   46
Road Map   47
Roman Statue   48

THE MIDDLE AGES   49

Racehorse   50
Gold-Leaf Sheet   51
Nazca Condor   52
Maya Cacao Bean   53

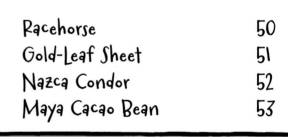

Ancient Briton   54
Clash Helmet   55
Viking   56
Female Emperor   58
Highly Inventive   59
Medieval Monk   60

Newsflash 61
Two Bronze Bowls 62
Sandstone Block 63
Bayeux Tapestry Maker 64
Robot Maker 66
Dead Sheep (Magna Carta) 67
Mongol Emperor 68
Māori Settler 69
Albatross (Rapa Nui) 70
Newsflash 71
Samurai Sword 72
Soapstone Bird 73
Aztec Skull 74
Temple of Doom 75
Plague Carrier 76
Press Express 77
Off the Chart! 78
Great Navigator 80

THE MODERN AGE 81

Wooden Board 82
Inca Farmer 84
Map Maker 85
Queen 86
Play Time 87
Mughal Artist 88
Newsflash 89
Powhatan Chief 90
Uninvited Guests 91
Astronomer 92
Tulip 93
Scientist's Cat 94
Newsflash 96
Pirate's Flag 97

Russian Beard 98
Kate the Great 99
Severed Head 100
Ship's Cat 101
Newsflash 102
Fossil Fuel 103
Mountain 104
Giant Tortoise 105
Star (Harriet Tubman) 106

Tragic Traffic 107
Microbe 108
Back to the Future 109
Newsflash 110
White Flower 111
Dog of War 112
Movie Writer 114
Flask of Soup 115
Letter 'V' 116
War and Peace 117
Stick of Chalk 118
Civil Rights 119
'Seagull' 120
Smartphone 121
Carbon Atom 122
The Future 123

GLOSSARY 124

ABOUT MIKE AND JESS 127

WHERE IN THE WORLD?

This map shows you all of the countries that feature in this book.
If you're unsure where a particular Day in the Life page
takes place, turn back to this map to find out.

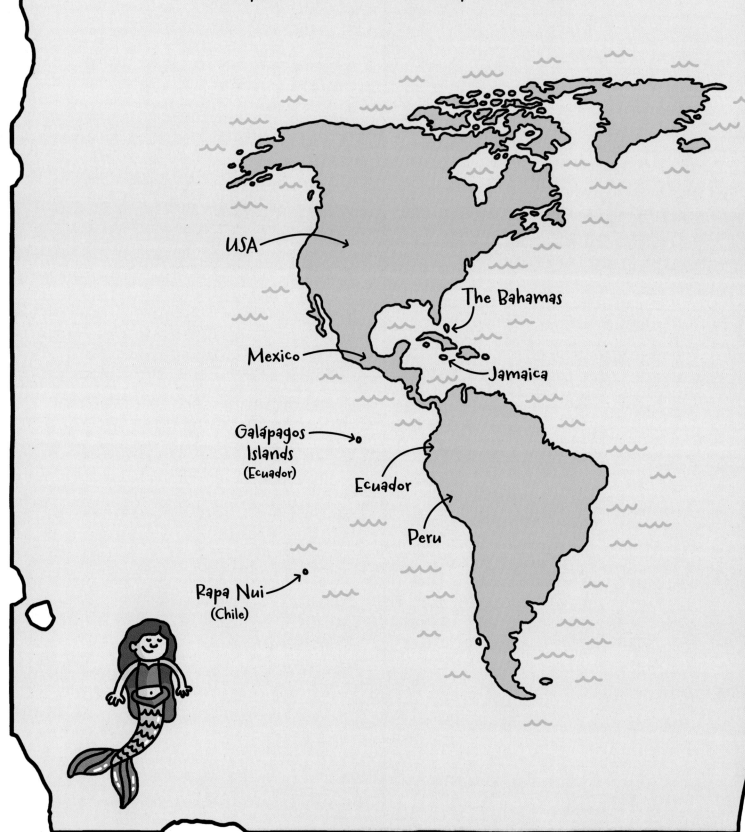

USA

The Bahamas

Mexico

Jamaica

Galápagos
Islands
(Ecuador)

Ecuador

Peru

Rapa Nui
(Chile)

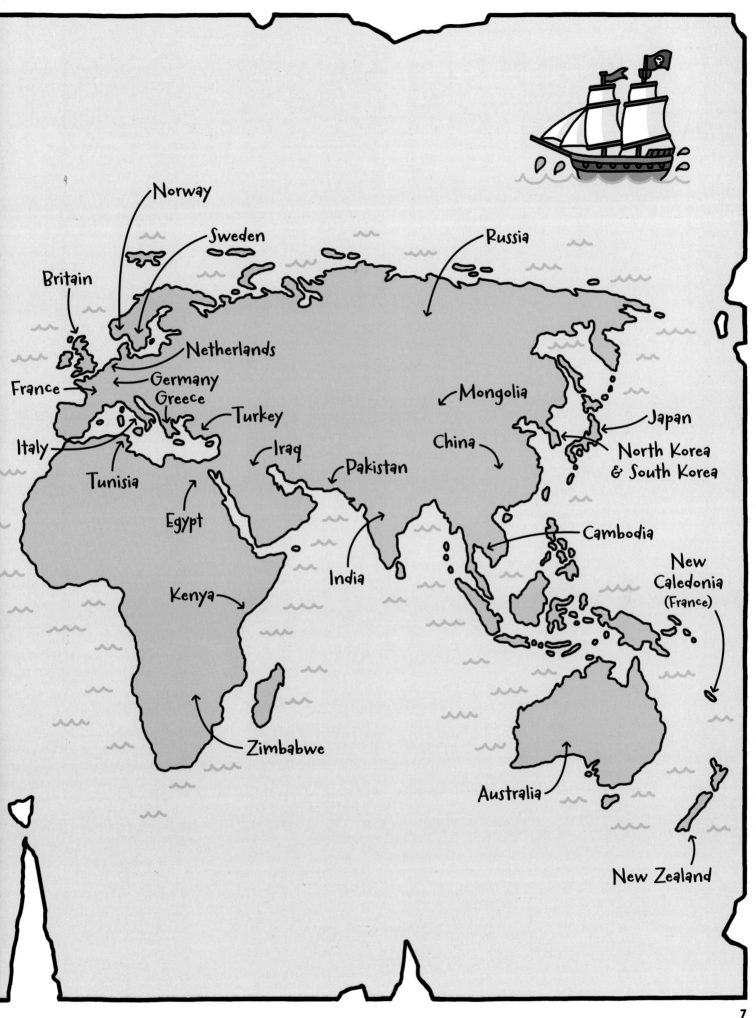

INTRODUCTION

Welcome to *A Day in the Life of a Caveman, a Queen and Everything in Between*. This book will take you on a tour through history as you've never seen it before.

It is split into three sections: Ancient History, The Middle Ages and The Modern Age. If you've ever wanted to know how the first wheel was invented, what life was like for a house in Pompeii and what a Galápagos tortoise thought of Charles Darwin, then look no further.

There are **Day in the Life** comics that give you a snapshot of different points in history, **Bigger Picture** pages that provide extra info, **Secret Diaries** that will let you into all sorts of inside knowledge, and **Newsflashes** to tell you what else was going on in the world at the time.

You'll also find a Glossary at the back of the book, which will help explain any tricky words you come across along the way.

So, what are you waiting for? Dive in. You haven't got all day!

ANCIENT HISTORY

The Earth is thought to be about 4.5 billion years old. Life began on our planet quite soon afterwards, but it was only about 6 million years ago – long after the dinosaurs had become extinct – that our first ancestors appeared in what we now call Africa. As they evolved into new species, our prehistoric relatives eventually spread across the planet – largely on foot.

Without written records, everything we know about the distant past comes from old relics and the work of archaeologists. A lot of ancient history remains a mystery. Time to find out more!

BCE AND CE
THE LETTERS 'BCE' AND 'CE' APPEAR AFTER THE DATES IN THIS CHAPTER. 'CE' STANDS FOR 'COMMON ERA', THE TIME WE LIVE IN NOW, WHERE MOST COUNTRIES SHARE THE SAME WAY OF DATING HISTORY. THIS STARTED AT THE YEAR 1 CE, JUST OVER 2,000 YEARS AGO. 'BCE' STANDS FOR 'BEFORE COMMON ERA' – THAT'S ALL THE YEARS BEFORE 1 CE, WHICH RUN BACKWARDS IN TIME. THERE WAS NO YEAR '0 CE' OR '0 BCE.'

A DAY IN THE LIFE OF ... HOMO ERECTUS

Hello! Welcome to what you now call Kenya, Africa, about 1.5 million years ago.

I'm *Homo erectus* – one of your ancient ancestors.

ME
HOMO ERECTUS

YOU
HOMO SAPIENS

Frankly, I think I look pretty good for my age, don't you?

- BIG SKULL
- EYEBROW RIDGES
- BIG TEETH
- LARGE FACE
- NO CHIN

Homo erectus means 'upright man'. That's because my species walked on two feet, unlike these apes here.

WE TRIED IT.

IT'S OVERRATED.

Your scientists know what we looked like from bits of our bones that they have found.

LONG THIGHBONES FOR STANDING UPRIGHT

THICK SKULLCAP WITH BROW RIDGES

BIG TEETH FOR CHEWING RAW FOOD

Using our long legs, we could run after animals for meat.

COME BACK!

NO WAY!

We then cut up this meat using our great, new, hi-tech invention ...

... the stone axe!

PAH! YOURS IS SO LAST YEAR.

SHARP

But this is our BEST discovery so far – fire! I've really warmed to it.

OI! WE'RE OFF TO SPREAD FROM AFRICA INTO EUROPE AND ASIA. YOU COMING?

SORRY, BUT I DON'T THINK WE SHOULD GO ...

WHY NOT?

WE HAVEN'T GOT A THING TO WEAR!

HOMO ERECTUS PROBABLY DIDN'T WEAR CLOTHES.

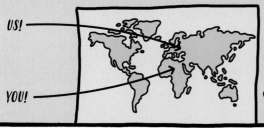

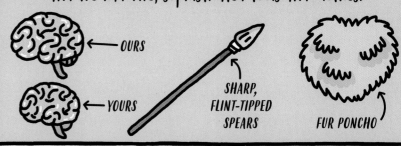

CAVEMAN

Hello, fellow human, and welcome to what you now call France about 30,000 years ago.

With the Neanderthals gone, we are the only human species left.

OOH, SCARY!

We're built a bit differently from Neanderthals, too.

- ROUNDER SKULL
- HIGHER FOREHEAD, NO BROW RIDGE
- SMALLER FACE AND NOSE
- CHIN
- SEWN FUR CLOTHES FOR LIFE IN COLDER PLACES
- LESS ROBUST SKELETON

Our species is called 'Homo sapiens', meaning 'wise man'.

CHOP!

AXE

WOOD

Hmm ... no comment.

AH, MY THUMB!

STONE TOOLS WERE STILL STATE OF THE ART.

Many early humans lived in caves – hence our nickname – often shared with scary wild animals. But we aren't all just 'cavemen' (or 'cavewomen') ...

BIT CROWDED IN HERE!

In fact, I'm a cave ARTIST!

Here are some examples of my handiwork. We make these hand stencils by blowing pigment over our hands.

We also paint pictures of large, wild animals, such as woolly rhinos and horses.

But you're probably wondering why we create these images? Well ...

PHUT

OOPS!

I'm afraid you'll have to remain in the dark! Nobody knows!

Cave paintings created by early humans are sometimes the only evidence we have of what long-lost animal species looked like. These animals – that are now all sadly extinct – can be seen painted on the walls of caves across Europe.

BIG CATS

Cave lions became extinct about 13,000 years ago and shared caves with early humans. Eek!

GIANT COWS

Aurochs were a species of wild cattle that died out by the 1600s.

EARLY RHINOS

Woolly rhinos locked horns in Europe and Asia over 10,000 years ago. They may have had black stripes round their middles.

ANCIENT DEER

These incredible antlers belong to an Irish elk – a giant deer that became extinct about 7,000 years ago.

MAGICAL BEAST

The identity of this strange spotted animal remains a mystery. It was painted in the Lascaux caves in France 17,000 years ago. Today, people call it 'the unicorn' – despite it having two horns!

The secret diary of a
WOOLLY MAMMOTH

The diary of Tina, a member of a herd of woolly mammoths in what is now Russia, 12,000 years ago.

'LITTLE ME'

DAY 1

Brr! Talk about an 'Ice Age'. Today was freezing. Glad of my long, woolly brown coat with its two layers of fur and my long tusks for sweeping the snow off the yummy grass underneath. Also secretly pleased to have a skin flap that keeps my rear warm. No mammoth wants a frozen bum, do they?

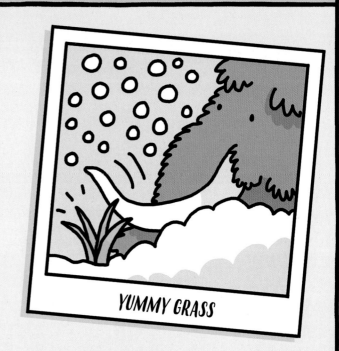

YUMMY GRASS

DAY 2

Tooth trouble! I was foraging with the herd when one of my four big molars fell out. I need those teeth to grind up the plants I pull up with my trunk. Then I remembered that we get six sets of teeth in our 60-year lives. Phew! I wonder if there is a mammoth tooth fairy – my molar could be worth a fortune.

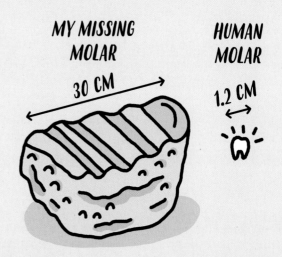

MY MISSING MOLAR
30 CM

HUMAN MOLAR
1.2 CM

DAY 3

Today, Mimi, the female mammoth who heads our herd, called me 'fat neck'. I blushed, as it is *such* a big compliment. We all store fat in humps just behind our heads, which gets us through winter when food is short AND it keeps us warm. No one loves a skinny mammoth!

MY LOVELY HUMP

PHEW!

DAY 4

Worryingly warm weather today. Not good when you're covered in thick fur. Someone in the herd muttered something about 'climate change' and how it might kill us all one day. But Mimi shut him up by hitting him with her tusks, thank goodness.

DAY 5

Those tiny humans can be SOOOO annoying. Several of them armed with spears tried to ambush me today. I've heard horror stories that they build shelters from our bones and skins, and carve tools out of our tusks. Luckily, I saw them coming and escaped. My fur may be woolly, but NOT my brain. So long, suckers!

ME

HUMANS MAKING A MAMMOTH MISTAKE

NEWSFLASH
Get the lowdown on what early humans were getting up to.

HOMO SAPIENS AT NO. 1
With the extinction of the Neanderthals, *Homo sapiens* (us) are the clear winners of the 'humans' race.

SETTLING DOWN
Farming develops around 9500 BCE. People stop wandering about in search of food and stay put – the beginnings of 'civilization'. The first great civilizations are those of ancient Egypt and an area called Mesopotamia.

INCREDIBLE INVENTIONS
Early humans can't stop inventing things. First bows and arrows, then farming, pottery, weaving and religious rituals. People also build stone structures, including thousands of 'dolmens' in Gojoseon (Korea), and the giant stone rows at Carnac in France.

AROUND 3,000 STONES WERE ERECTED IN CARNAC BETWEEN 4500 BCE AND 3300 BCE.

BATH TIME
In the Indus Valley in modern-day Pakistan, a civilization develops with water and hygiene at its heart. Sadly, it disappears by 1700 BCE.

MUCH MORE CIVILIZED
The invention of metal tools means that stone and wood can be worked more skilfully. Early forms of writing, such as hieroglyphs, also give us our first real historical records – provided you can decipher them!

TWO OWLS? WHAT A HOOT!

A DAY IN THE LIFE OF A ...

FARMER

Hello! Welcome to Sumer in Mesopotamia, around 4000 BCE. I'm an early farmer.

Very bloomin' early – it's only just gone dawn. It gets so hot here in the day, we have to start work sharpish.

— HOT!

Before humans invented farming, we had to find food in the wild and were known as 'hunter-gatherers'.

I GATHER YOU'RE A HUNTER?

NO, I'M A HUNTER-GATHERER!

Farming meant that we could stay in one place rather than go searching for food.

THANK GOODNESS FOR THAT!

WE AGREE!

These are some of the first things us humans farmed ...

GRAPES

SHEEP

DATES

OLIVES

BLISTERS (IT'S HARD WORK!)

Barley, a cereal, is also very important. It was developed from a wild grass.

DON'T EAT ME – I'M IMPORTANT!

We use barley to make bread and beer.

Because it's so hot and dry here ...

GASP!

WE COULD DO WITH A COLD DRINK, TOO!

... we invented a way to get water from the rivers to the fields, known as 'irrigation'.

AH, THAT'S BETTER!

Plus, we invented the plough and fish farming.

EARLY PLOUGH

I'm not sure we've got the hang of that last one yet ...

WHEEL

Hey! Ever feel you spend all your time going round in circles?

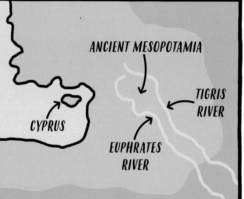

I certainly do!

I'm a wooden wheel on a chariot in Mesopotamia around 3000 BCE.

CLIP, CLOP!

ME TOO!

'Mesopotamia' is an area between the Euphrates and Tigris rivers, in modern-day Iraq. It's where humans built the first cities.

ANCIENT MESOPOTAMIA

TIGRIS RIVER

CYPRUS

EUPHRATES RIVER

NORTH AFRICA

Being an early wheel, I'm simply two semi-circles of wood with an axle in the centre.

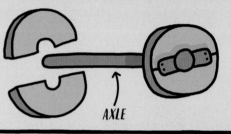

AXLE

Despite this, I was literally a 'revolutionary' idea – geddit?

NO, SORRY.

For some reason, it took ages for you humans to invent us.

And the first wheels were probably used to make pots.

CLAY POT

FANCY A SPIN?

It may be that some people had the idea earlier. Us wheels do get around. The oldest-known wheel was found in Slovenia.

I'M 5,150 YEARS OLD!

To be honest, I don't care who thought of us first.

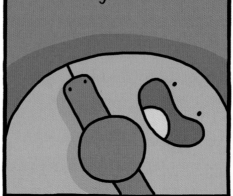

I just wish you'd hurry up and invent the tyre – these rocks hurt!

OW!

BUMP!

STANDING STONE

Hi there. Welcome to Salisbury Plain in Britain, around 2100 BCE. I'm a member of a famous rock group.

Stonehenge!

'Henge' is an old word that means 'hanging' – and I do a lot of hanging about, frankly.

4 METRES TALL

← 2 METRES WIDE →

COOEE!

Us upright stones are called 'sarsens' and that lazy lump up there is a 'lintel'.

Let me tell you, it's no fun standing here for years with a 22,000 kg weight on your head.

NOT MY FAULT!

TCH! HEART OF STONE, THAT ONE ...

I was happier being part of a big seam of sandstone in a quarry about 30 kilometres away.

CHIP!

OW! THAT HURTS!

Neolithic humans used flint axes and wedges to work me into shape. Talk about a 'splitting' headache!

After that, how I got to this windy plain (and why) remains a mystery to me ...

... and to modern archaeologists!

All we know for sure is that twice a year, a special stone called the Heel Stone gets blinded by the sunrise.

THE HEEL STONE

DON'T WORRY, MATES. I'VE GOT THIS SORTED!

APPARENTLY, WINTER'S COMING ...

BETTER PUT SOME MORE FUR ON ...

STONEHENGE WAS POSSIBLY USED AS A GIANT CALENDAR TO TRACK THE MOVEMENT OF THE SUN.

A DAY IN THE LIFE OF AN ... INDUS BACTERIUM

Grrr! I'm a nasty microbe in a sewer in the Indus Valley region in what you call Pakistan.

MAGNIFIED ABOUT 10,000 TIMES

It's about 2000 BCE and there's something bugging all of us bad bacteria.

TOO RIGHT!

This city we're in is a total 'mare for microbes!

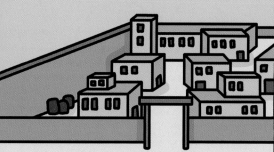

THE ANCIENT CITY OF MOHENJO-DARO WAS MADE UP OF BRICK BUILDINGS ON A REGULAR GRID PATTERN. AS MANY AS 40,000 PEOPLE MAY HAVE LIVED HERE.

It's ahead of its time in terms of hygiene.

US WATERBORNE BUGS ARE STRUGGLING TO THRIVE!

GASP!

This is the squeaky-clean region I'm talking about ...

MODERN-DAY PAKISTAN
INDUS VALLEY
ARABIAN SEA
MODERN-DAY INDIA

The people who live here are horribly keen on keeping clean.

DIRT WON'T WASH WITH US!

They've even built giant public baths.

EVERY NIGHT IS BATH NIGHT!

I BROUGHT MY DUCKY!

QUACK!

This city alone has 700 wells supplying clean water ...

WELL WORTH LOOKING INTO ...

... and homes have their own loos!

A LITTLE PRIVACY, PLEASE?

Not only that, each loo is flushed with a jar of clean water.

INTO THE GREAT UNKNOWN WE GO!

The poo from each loo travels safely away down brick-built covered sewers.

WHEEEEEEE!

DON'T YOU MEAN, 'POOOOOOO'?

It's just not fair on all us bacteria that like to cause diseases.

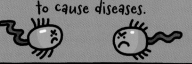

LOOK, WILL YOU PLEASE JUST LEAVE ME ALONE?!

MICRONESIAN BIRD

I'm a *Sylviornis* – a giant, flightless bird related to the chicken.

1.7 METRES TALL

Hello. It's about 1500 BCE. Welcome to a remote island paradise in the Pacific Ocean that you call New Caledonia.

Well, it was a paradise until you humans turned up.

And these people are settlers from mainland Asia. They've been travelling across vast stretches of water in boats to islands like mine.

I SPY LAND!

I SPY DANGER!

This clever invention is called the outrigger canoe, and it got you humans across the oceans.

CRAB-CLAW SAIL

FLOAT, OR 'OUTRIGGER', FOR SUPPORT

PADDLE OARS

Me, I'm a total birdbrain, but you humans are super sailors!

You can read the waves and use 'stick charts' to find your way.

SHELLS REPRESENT ISLANDS

STICKS SHOW OCEAN PATTERNS

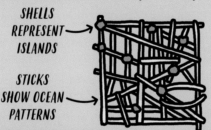

Here on my island, humans have made some lovely pots.

GEOMETRIC DESIGNS ARE POPULAR.

HISTORIANS CALL THIS SOCIETY THE 'LAPITA CULTURE'.

I just wish you hadn't brought this horrible lot with you. They attack our nests, eggs and chicks.

PIGS

WILD DOGS

RATS

It's bad enough with you humans hunting us for food!

YUM.

OOPS! MUST FLY!

HELP! I FORGOT ... I CAN'T FLY. EEK!

SADLY, *SYLVIORNIS* WAS HUNTED TO EXTINCTION BY THE LAPITA SETTLERS.

EGYPTIAN PHARAOH

Welcome to the city of Thebes, around 1465 BCE.

I'm the pharaoh Hatshepsut, and here's an odd thing ...

... I'm a woman! In fact, I'm only the second female pharaoh so far.

FAKE BEARD

I like to think ahead. Look at the amazing temple I'm building in the Valley of the Kings for when I'm dead. It's huge!

I was one of the greatest builders of ancient Egypt. I just *love* building things!

GIANT STONE OBELISK (OR PILLAR) IN KARNAK, EGYPT

LIFE-SIZE STATUE OF ME

ME AS A SPHINX!

I'm able to do all this because my husband the king died, leaving me free rein to reign.

MY HUSBAND, THUTMOSE II

Not that my young stepson, Thutmose III, is keen on the idea ...

WOMEN DON'T RULE AS A RULE IN ANCIENT EGYPT.

Despite being a woman, I can still dress as a king.

COBRA ORNAMENT ('URAEUS')

STRIPED 'NEMES' HEADDRESS

FAKE BEARD ('POSTICHE')

I also get to have my name carved in stone everywhere! My name means 'most notable of noble women'.

JUST CARVE 'HATSHEPSUT'!

THAT'S EASY FOR YOU TO SAY ...

Thanks to me, Egypt is peaceful and prosperous ... and my name will live on forever.

HMM ... WE SHALL SEE.

After my death in 1458 BCE, Thutmose III had many of my statues destroyed. My existence wasn't discovered until the 19th century.

OH NO! I'VE LOST FACE!

The ancient Egyptians developed hieroglyphs in around 3000 BCE. This early form of writing used symbols and pictures to represent actual objects, as well as ideas and sounds, a bit like a modern alphabet. Hieroglyphs were painted on to a material made from plants, called papyrus, or carved on to walls.

THIS IS HOW THE NAME OF THE ANCIENT EGYPTIAN QUEEN CLEOPATRA WAS WRITTEN IN HIEROGLYPHS. THE OVAL FRAME THAT SURROUNDS THE HIEROGLYPHS IS CALLED A 'CARTOUCHE'.

THE ROSETTA STONE

In 1799, a stone was discovered in the Egyptian town of Rosetta. A piece of text had been copied on to it in two forms of ancient Egyptian writing (hieroglyphs and a script called 'demotic') as well as in Greek. This allowed historians to translate hieroglyphs for the first time.

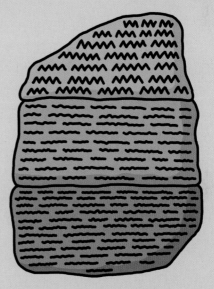

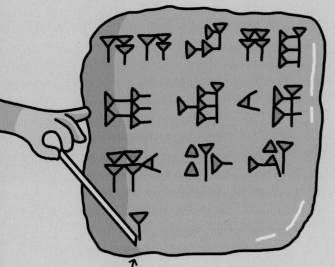

INCREDIBLE CUNEIFORM

The world's first-known writing system was created in 3200 BCE by the Sumerian people of Mesopotamia. It was known as cuneiform and contained hundreds of different symbols.

CUNEIFORM SYMBOLS WERE MADE BY PRESSING A REED INTO WET CLAY.

The secret diary of an EGYPTIAN CAT

The diary of a stray cat in the ancient Egyptian city of Heliopolis around 1450 BCE.

ME!

DAY 1

Cats certainly DO always land on their feet. Yesterday, I was a stray. Today, I've been welcomed into a human family's home. Already, they have named me 'Miu' and fed me a fish head! I'm being treated like a little furry god.

FISH HEAD — A DELICACY!

OLD MIU

DAY 2

Oops. Seems like they have another cat — also called Miu — who is much older than me. Old Miu says they call all us cats 'Miu' after the noise we make. They also consider us so special that any human who kills a cat gets sentenced to death. Now who reckons a dog is man's best friend?! Not me!

DAY 3

Me and Old Miu went hunting today and took out three mice, two rats, a scorpion AND a cobra. Old Miu says this is why humans love us so much – we keep them safe. Frankly, I don't care why – just keep the fish heads coming!

MUMMIFIED
OLD MIU

DAY 4

Tragedy! Poor Old Miu has battled his last cobra. Our humans are so upset they have shaved off their eyebrows in a show of mourning. They have also had Old Miu's body covered in oils and wrapped in bandages like a mummy. He does look funny. I wonder why they have done it?

DAY 5

Long journey today to a temple dedicated to a cat-headed goddess called Bastet. Seems Old Miu is going to spend the afterlife here, along with hundreds of other dead cats, all in jars or coffins. I'll miss him – but I got lots of cuddles and I'm sure the humans will be happy again once their eyebrows grow back. Miaow!

BASTET, GODDESS OF THE HOME,
CATS AND CHILDBIRTH

NEWSFLASH

By 1500 BCE, humans are certainly going places, and not just by land.

ARRIVING IN AUSTRALIA

During the last Ice Age, the sea level was much lower than it is in modern times, shortening the distances between islands. By 1500 BCE, people have already been living in Australia for 50,000 years, and further exploration is on the way.

COASTLINES IN ICE AGE OCEANIA SHOWN IN PINK

BIGGER HORIZONS

New boat technology allows brave men and women to sail to and explore remote Pacific islands. Though this is not always to the benefit of local wildlife.

AWESOME ART

In Central and South America, early empires form that we're only aware of today thanks to a few fragments of pottery and some incredible art.

LEAVING A LEGACY

It may sound potty, but in both Korea and Greece civilizations come and go whose presence is recorded largely on jugs, jars and other ceramics. The ancient Greeks leave a legacy that includes science, art, philosophy, drama, sport and even history itself.

LLAMA

Humans took the wild type and made it so much calmer.*

A MEMBER OF THE CAMEL FAMILY

EARS UP = HAPPY
EARS FLAT = CROSS

LONG, SOFT FUR

*A PROCESS CALLED 'DOMESTICATION'.

Hi! We're in Ecuador, him and me ...

... ROUND ABOUT 1500 BCE.

I'm a llama.

AND I'M A LLAMA FARMER.

Historians call our society the 'Valdivia Culture'.

THATCHED ROOF

CIRCULAR MUD WALLS

LLAMA PADDOCK

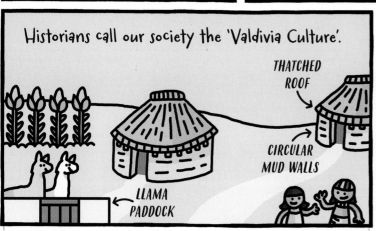

It was big on weaving cotton and certain types of sculpture.

COTTON PLANT

PARROT POTTERY

VENUS FIGURE

COTTON CLOTH

Llamas in Valdivia have so much work to do ...

We carry things ...

You weave our wool ...

SHORT, BACK AND SIDES, PLEASE.

... and even burn our poo!

When it comes to being helpful, a llama's hard to beat ...

ALSO TRUE.

... AND DON'T TELL HER, BUT LLAMA MEAT IS ALSO NICE TO EAT!

WHAT?!

3,500 YEARS LATER ...

US LLAMAS STILL DO THESE THINGS IN MODERN TIMES.

AND US LLAMAS STILL LOVE TO BUST SOME RHYMES!

OLMEC HEAD

Hello! I'm a giant boulder in a city in what you now call Mexico. It's about 1200 BCE.

Well, I say 'boulder' ...

... I'm actually now a huge sculpture created by a culture your historians call the Olmec.

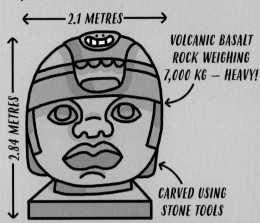

← 2.1 METRES →

2.84 METRES

VOLCANIC BASALT ROCK WEIGHING 7,000 KG — HEAVY!

CARVED USING STONE TOOLS

'OLMEC' MEANS 'RUBBER PEOPLE'. THE OLMEC EXTRACTED RUBBER FROM TREES.

The Olmec have built cities with statues, pyramids and water systems, creating Mexico's first great civilization.

GIANT SCULPTURES OF HEADS MAY HAVE LINED SPECIAL WALKWAYS

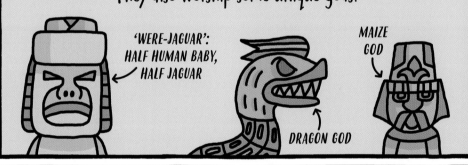

They also worship some unique gods!

'WERE-JAGUAR': HALF HUMAN BABY, HALF JAGUAR

DRAGON GOD

MAIZE GOD

Maize (sweetcorn) has made the Olmec wealthy. No wonder they worship it!

WE'RE SOLID GOLD, WE ARE!

The Olmec also play lots of games using a heavy rubber ball, made using tree sap.

IT WEIGHS UP TO 4 KG!

Your historians reckon I'm wearing a helmet used by ball-game players. Well, let me tell you a secret ...

DONK!

OI! THAT BALL HURTS!

MUMUN JAR

Welcome to the kingdom of Gojoseon – in what you call Korea – in about 700 BCE.

HI!

As you can see, I'm a big brown jar and he's a little grey pot.

WE'VE JUST BEEN MADE!

Legend has it that the kingdom of Gojoseon was founded by a god-king called Dangun, whose mum was a bear. The story is still celebrated in Korea today.

HAPPY MOTHER'S DAY!

THANK YOU, SON.

Yes, well, right now this house we're living in is the pits.

LITERALLY.

Half of it is underground!

THATCHED ROOF

ENTRANCE

BELOW-GROUND LIVING SPACE

'Pit-houses' are typical of the Mumun period. The period is named after us pots.

The people who live in this house fish, forage and use stone and bronze tools.

HALF-MOON-SHAPED STONE KNIFE

MANDOLIN-SHAPED BRONZE DAGGER

They also grow lots of crops.

BARLEY

MILLET

WHEAT

Plus this very useful one.

I'M RICE AND I'M NICE!

RICE WAS FIRST GROWN IN ASIA IN ABOUT 6000 BCE.

I WONDER WHAT I'LL BE USED TO STORE?

I THINK YOU'RE ABOUT TO FIND OUT!

LATER ...

Human body parts – yuk!

I'm now a coffin jar in a burial chamber under an arrangement of rocks called a 'dolmen'. Only rich, powerful people were buried like this.

ROCK SLABS

BAD LUCK!

I'M DYING TO ESCAPE!

GREEK VASE

Hello! I'm a brand-new shiny vase in a pottery shop in Athens around 530 BCE.

I used to be just a lump of clay.

BABY PICTURE

But look at me now ... I'm a beautiful vase called an 'amphora', used for storing wine, oil or honey.

THE PICTURE ON ME SHOWS TWO FIGURES FROM GREEK MYTHOLOGY PLAYING A BOARD GAME.

I was made on a potter's wheel before I had this design painted on me.

DIZZY!

That tickled, but the worst part was being fired in the kiln ... three times!

IS IT ME OR IS IT HOT IN HERE?

PHEW!

Some pottery makers – mine included – sign their work. Just look at my bottom!

'MADE BY EXEKIAS'

Us pots provide an important record of life in ancient Greece. We show gods, myths, Olympic heroes and daily life.

ZEUS, GREEK GOD   SAILING BOATS   OLYMPIC RACERS   BUILDINGS   BATTLES

Styles have changed over the years.

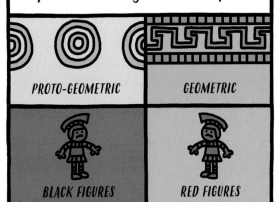

PROTO-GEOMETRIC

GEOMETRIC

BLACK FIGURES

RED FIGURES

But pots are SO popular. This shop gets really busy. Oops! Look out!

BUMP!

OI – WATCH IT!

COME BACK!

WOBBLE!

HELP!

ARE YOU OK?

I'M SHATTERED! SOB!

As well as making amazing pottery, the ancient Greeks were also skilled sculptors. Some of their surviving statues are among the world's best-known works of art.

ARTEMISION BRONZE

This statue dates to 460 BCE. It is thought to show Zeus, the king of the gods. Originally, he would have been holding a lightning bolt.

LIGHTNING BOLT HOLE

HIS EYES ARE MISSING!

OVER 2 METRES TALL!

VENUS DE MILO

The Venus de Milo was carved from marble in about 100 BCE and probably shows Aphrodite, the Greek goddess of love. The statue was found on the Greek island of Milos in 1820, hence the name. No one knows why her arms are missing.

OVER 2 METRES TALL!

THE DISCOBOLUS

This discus thrower was created by Myron, a famous Athenian sculptor, in about 460 BCE. It now only exists through copies made by the Romans.

DISCUS THROWING WAS AN EVENT IN THE ANCIENT OLYMPICS. THE DISCUS USED IN THE GAMES WOULD HAVE BEEN MADE OF STONE, BRONZE OR IRON.

 A DAY IN THE LIFE OF AN ...

ANCIENT OLYMPIAN

 Hi! I'm a citizen living in the town of Olympia, Greece, in the year 460 BCE.

AS AM I.

 Thousands of people have come to our town from all over Greece for the start of another Olympiad.

HAPPENS EVERY FOUR YEARS.

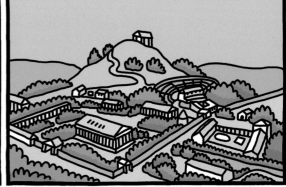 The games are held in honour of the god Zeus. And what an incredible sight Olympia is right now.

 Amazing to think that the first games back in 776 BCE had just one event ...

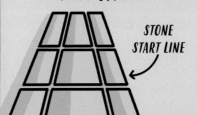 ... a 190-metre-long running race called the 'stadion' – from where you get the word 'stadium'.

STONE START LINE

 Olympic champions get a crown of laurels ...

... and their faces on lots of vases!

Nowadays, there are many more events ...

 DISCUS THROWING

 JAVELIN THROWING

 RUNNING IN ARMOUR

 PANKRATION — A MIX OF BOXING AND WRESTLING

 None of which involve women, either as competitors or spectators.

WOMEN WEREN'T ALLOWED TO TAKE PART.

 Now, let's go and meet one of the athletes down at the track ...

GREAT IDEA!

 TRACKSIDE ...

GOOD LUCK — BUT YOU DO KNOW EVERYONE COMPETES NAKED?

WHAT? NO WAY!

 WELL, HE CAN CERTAINLY RUN VERY FAST.

AARGH! FLEE!

ALL THE ATHLETES WERE NUDE!

HISTORIAN

Welcome to Athens! It's about 430 BCE. My name is Herodotus of Halicarnassus, but you can call me ...

... SUPERHERO! I'm the world's first famous historian.

It's thanks to me that you know about the Mesopotamian city of Babylon, renowned for its 'Hanging Gardens'.

I wrote all about Babylon in a book called *The Histories*, which still survives in your day.

'THE HISTORIES' BY HERODOTUS

Admittedly, I may have got a few 'facts' wrong.

HERODOTUS: BABYLON HAD 100 BRONZE CITY GATES.

ACTUAL: BABYLON HAD JUST EIGHT CITY GATES.

But look what's left of it in your time.

THE RUINS OF BABYLON ARE IN MODERN-DAY IRAQ.

That's why my record of the ancient world is important. I travel and collect information that will otherwise be forgotten about.

I've also written about lots of famous battles ...

TAKE THAT! AND YOU!

MARATHON c.490 BCE (GREEKS VS PERSIANS)

HELLO AGAIN. HOW ARE YOU DOING?

THERMOPYLAE c.480 BCE (GREEKS VS PERSIANS)

SAME TIME NEXT YEAR? WHY NOT!

MYCALE c.479 BCE (GREEKS VS PERSIANS)

And I throw in some weird stuff, too.

GLITTER! DIG! EEK!

Herodotus claimed that a giant, furry Persian ant dug up gold dust. And the ant could also kill a camel!

Still, on the whole, much of my work has been shown to be accurate and I'm known as the 'father of history'.

NO. 1 DAD

And that's the truth!

WELL, MORE OR LESS ...

The secret diary of a
MASK MAKER

The diary of Jason, an apprentice at a theatre near Athens in about 430 BCE.

ME!

DAY 1

Went to meet Cyril, the man I hope will be my teacher for the next few years. Cyril makes all the clothes and masks for the actors in Athens' big theatre. There are two main types of play – 'tragedies' (serious) and 'comedies' (funny). Cyril offered me an apprenticeship and I start tomorrow. Success!

CYRIL

DAY 2

Cyril showed me around my new workplace. Banks of wooden seats form a semi-circle cut into the hillside – a shape that allows all 10,000 people in the audience to hear the actors clearly. Cyril says the seats are called the 'theatron' and the stage is known as the 'orchestra'. So many new words!

DAY 3

Today, Cyril showed me the masks he has in his workshop – complete with wigs made from real human hair. Apparently, the many different masks disguise the fact that no play has more than three main actors. All of the actors are men. Sadly, women aren't allowed in the theatre, meaning my mum can't come and watch. Boo!

THE SKENE

DAY 4

Cyril took me inside a little tent they have on stage where the actors change their masks during the performance. Sometimes, it also has a picture on it of a setting. The tent is called a 'skene', so I joked with Cyril that they could call those background pictures 'skenery'. He just looked at me like I was crazy. Oh well.

DAY 5

I've made my first mask! I pressed stiffened cloth on to a mould and added holes for the eyes and mouth. 'Well done,' said Cyril. 'Now, make eleven more!' He wasn't joking. The masks are worn by the chorus – 12 actors who all speak the same lines together and wear identical masks. All 12 masks were smiling – unlike me at the end of the day. But I mustn't make a drama out of it.

GREEK PHILOSOPHER

Hello. My name is Plato. It's about 360 BCE – and I'm a really famous brainbox. But, never forget ...

... I used to be a wrestler! Grr!

TRUE – HE WAS.

Now I run a school in Athens called 'the Academy' where all the cleverest people can come to learn and argue in a beautiful grove of olive trees.

I'M NOT SURE I AGREE, PLATO.

CAREFUL! I USED TO BE A WRESTLER.

We call boffins like me 'philosophers'. 'Philosophy' comes from two Greek words meaning 'love of wisdom'.

CHOMP! CHOMP!

Different philosophers have different ideas ...

SOCRATES

I SAID BEING GOOD WAS ENOUGH TO MAKE YOU HAPPY. HONEST.

DEMOCRITUS

I CAME UP WITH THE IDEA OF ATOMS.

DIOGENES

I LIVED IN A GIANT CLAY JAR!

Many were also very good at maths – including me!

TETRAHEDRON   CUBE   OCTAHEDRON   ICOSAHEDRON

THESE 3D SHAPES ARE KNOWN AS 'PLATONIC SOLIDS' TODAY.

The philosopher Pythagoras also had a famous bit of maths named after him.

THESE SQUARES MADE ME HIP!

A = B + C
BY AREA:
$A = B + C$

However, here at the Academy, this is my star pupil – Aristotle.

THANK YOU!

YOU FLATTER ME, MASTER. HOWEVER, WHEREAS YOU BELIEVE THOUGHT ALONE IS ENOUGH TO REVEAL TRUTH, I CONSIDER ONLY DIRECT OBSERVATION CAN REVEAL IT. WHAT DO YOU SAY TO THAT?

HMMM ...

WRESTLE!

NEWSFLASH

The period between 500 BCE and 500 CE sees empires rise – and fall.

AGE OF EMPIRES

Powerful rulers and even more powerful armies spread their territories across the known world, along with their technology, beliefs and ways of life. Indeed, for the ancient Romans, roaming from home becomes their main occupation.

LASTING LEGACY

In China, previously warring states are brought together under the control of Qin Shi Huang, who becomes the nation's first emperor. Qin's dynasty doesn't last, but the wall he started to build is still with us today!

ALL ROADS LEAD TO

Rome, a small hilly city in what is now Italy, ends up creating one of the greatest empires ever. It lasts for over 1,000 years and it is said 'all roads lead to Rome'. In Roman times, this included the Silk Road, which cut across continents from the Mediterranean Sea to China.

THE FALL OF ROME

It is said that 'Rome wasn't built in a day'. However, an invading army takes just three days to rob the city in 410 CE. Rome's days of glory are numbered and the Roman Empire eventually collapses in 476 CE.

CHINESE EMPEROR

We're in Pingyuan in China in 210 BCE. How dare you look at me?! This is an outrage!

Kneel as you read this! Don't you know who I am?

TOSS! SWALLOW!

I am his Imperial Majesty Qin Shi Huang – head of the Qin Dynasty and first emperor of China.

TOSS! SWALLOW!

POISONOUS MERCURY PILLS

In 221 BCE, I unified all seven warring states – including my own – making me the first emperor.

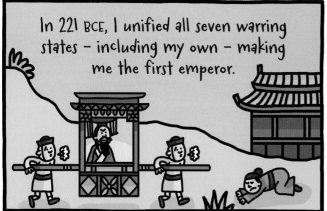

I also began the building of the Great Wall in the north of China. At first, it was just made of mud, stones and, sometimes, rice.

WHAT DO YOU THINK OF IT SO FAR?

GOOD, BUT NOT 'GREAT' ...

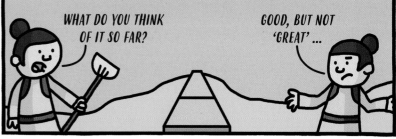

I also built roads and canals, and I made weights and words the same across all of China.

MEASURING SPOON

People claim that I had hundreds of scholars put to death (and their books burnt) because they didn't believe in magic ... the fools!

Err, maybe forget about that bit.

I'm currently having a huge tomb built for when I die.

NICE SPOT TO BE BURIED ...

MOUNT LI

But I'm not going to die, thanks to all these magic 'elixir of life' pills I've been taking. Ha!

TOSS! SWALLOW!

Oops! Maybe I'm wrong ...

WE DON'T KNOW THE CAUSE OF QIN SHI HUANG'S DEATH, BUT HE WAS POSSIBLY POISONED BY THE PILLS HE THOUGHT WOULD MAKE HIM IMMORTAL.

FEAT OF CLAY

Qin Shi Huang's city-sized tomb was discovered by accident in 1974. Inside was a whole army of over 8,000 life-size figures to protect him in the afterlife. They were all made from a clay called terracotta and are known today as the 'Terracotta Army'.

THE FIGURES WERE MADE USING MOULDS, BUT DESPITE THIS NO TWO ARE IDENTICAL.

REAL WEAPONS WERE ADDED TO THE FIGURES.

THE FIGURES WERE ORIGINALLY BRIGHTLY PAINTED.

THE TOMB ALSO INCLUDES LIFE-SIZE HORSES.

DYE WHELK

Carthage is part of a Mediterranean civilization called 'Phoenicia'. The Phoenicians are great traders and sailors.

Hi! I'm a type of sea snail called a whelk. 'Whelk-come' to the city of Carthage in the year 220 BCE.

Though, frankly, I'd call this place 'carnage' – as we're all going to die.

EH?!

EUROPE

TYRE

CARTHAGE

AFRICA

ORANGE = PHOENICIAN EMPIRE

The Phoenicians' most valuable export is a bright fabric dye called 'Tyrian purple', named after the city of Tyre.

The dye is worth its weight in gold – literally!

HI! CAN I BUY DYE?

AYE!

GOLD

It's so expensive that it is reserved for the clothes of rich people and emperors.

HI!

WE'RE POSH PURPLE PEOPLE!

Trouble is, to make just a tiny amount of this dye, thousands of whelks have to die.

CAN YOU PLEASE STOP SAYING 'DIE'?!

We're crushed to death in tanks, boiled and then left to rot for days.

THIS JOB STINKS!

Different species of whelks produce slightly different shades.

And wool dipped in these dyes doesn't fade in sunlight, making it prized across continents.

OOH! IT STILL DOESN'T HALF ITCH, THOUGH.

I know all this because I read it on that skin on the wall.

WOW! YOU CAN READ? THAT'S UNBELIEVABLE!

THE PHOENICIANS DEVELOPED ONE OF THE WORLD'S EARLIEST ALPHABETS.

NOW TO MAKE A QUICK GETAWAY ...

GOOD LUCK!

HALF AN HOUR LATER ...

HMM, NOT EASY FOR A SNAIL ...

KEEP GOING!

WAR ELEPHANT

Welcome to northern Italy in December, 218 BCE. I'm a war elephant and I'm feeling pretty grumpy to be honest.

'Come on a trip to Italy,' they said. 'It'll be fun ...'

TUSK-SWORD

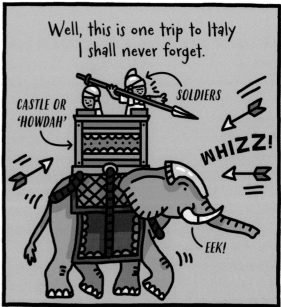

Well, this is one trip to Italy I shall never forget.

CASTLE OR 'HOWDAH'

SOLDIERS

WHIZZ!

EEK!

It's all this man's fault.

HANNIBAL BARCA
247 BCE–c.181 BCE

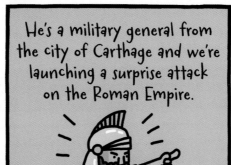

He's a military general from the city of Carthage and we're launching a surprise attack on the Roman Empire.

TIPPY!

TIPPY!

I thought 'surprise' meant everyone walking on tiptoe.

It actually meant me and 36 other elephants walking with his army all the way from Spain – 1,600 kilometres.

ROME

ALPS

SPAIN

HANNIBAL'S ROUTE

ITALY

Including crossing the Italian Alps.

I'M COLD ...

I'M HUNGRY ...

I'M SCARED OF HEIGHTS!

The Roman army uses fire to try to frighten us elephants.

To be honest, I'm just glad of the warmth. Why did we have to come here in winter?

HELP!

FALL!

We won the battle, but only one elephant survived ... me. Ah-choo!

41

GLADIATOR

Hello. Welcome to Rome, Italy, about 90 CE. Fancy a job entertaining people?

Have mine! I'm a gladiator at the Colosseum in Rome.

KILL HIM!

DIE, LOSER!

Tough crowd!

I'm a type of gladiator called a 'retiarius' (or 'net man').

SHARP TRIDENT

ARMOURED ARM

LARGE NET

BARE CHEST

No helmet, you'll notice, and I have to fight this guy to the death.

MUMBLE, MUMBLE, MUMBLE ...

BIG METAL HELMET

SORRY. I SAID, 'I'M A SECUTOR AND THIS SHORT SWORD IS A "GLADIUS" – FROM WHERE WE GET THE NAME GLADIATOR.'

I don't know who came up with these crazy costumes, but there are lots of them ...

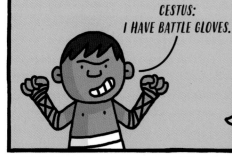

CESTUS: I HAVE BATTLE GLOVES.

MURMILLO: I HAVE A FISH-SHAPED HELMET.

HOPLOMACHUS: I HAVE A SHORT SPEAR.

COWARDUS*: I HAVE A NOTE FROM MY MUM.

*MAY NOT BE GENUINE

Most gladiators are enslaved people or criminals, and we don't usually live for more than ten fights.

YOU TWO ARE ON NEXT!

Well, people say the important thing is to die bravely. SIGH!

MUMBLE!*

*I HATE THIS JOB!

LATER ...

THEY SAY HE DIED BRAVELY ...

RIP

THUMBS DOWN TO THAT!

FIGHT SCHOOL

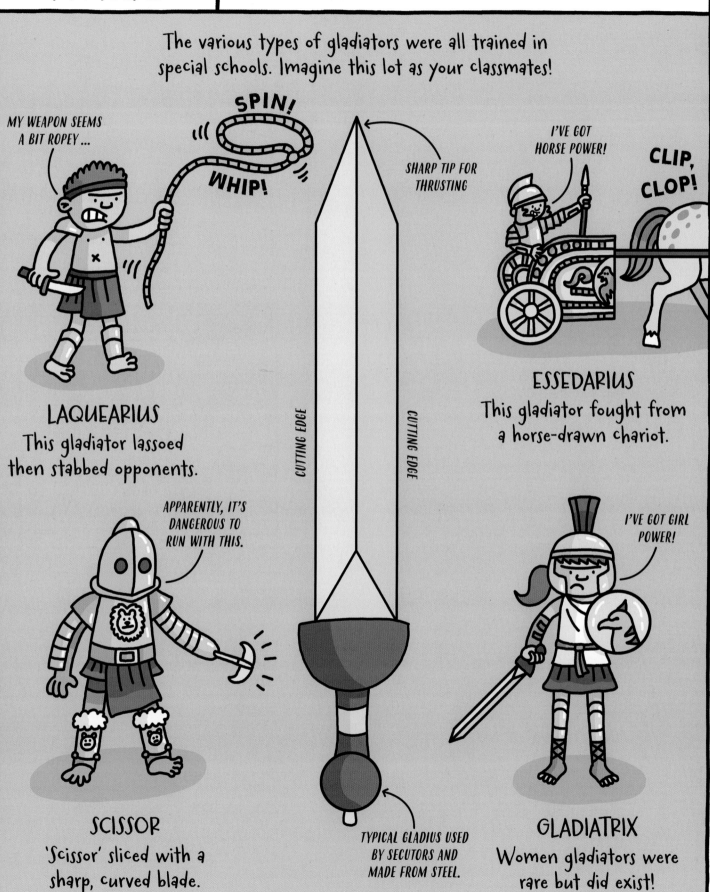

The various types of gladiators were all trained in special schools. Imagine this lot as your classmates!

LAQUEARIUS
This gladiator lassoed then stabbed opponents.

SCISSOR
'Scissor' sliced with a sharp, curved blade.

ESSEDARIUS
This gladiator fought from a horse-drawn chariot.

GLADIATRIX
Women gladiators were rare but did exist!

43

The secret diary of a
HOUSE IN POMPEII

The diary of Dom, a house or 'domus' in the Roman city of Pompeii, Italy, in 79 CE.

MY OUTSIDE

DAY 1

What a week! They say 'walls have ears' – and they're right. Today, a couple walked past on the street outside and said how dull I looked. Well, frankly, so do all the other houses in Pompeii from the outside. But, inside, I'm gorgeous – check out my picture! I've got pillars, a courtyard, a garden, statues, paintings and even a water feature.

MY GLORIOUS INSIDE

DAY 2

After yesterday's insult, how nice to have someone come in today to touch up my frescoes. Frescoes are colourful paintings on the walls of my rooms. My owners think themselves quite highbrow, so my frescoes are of battles and mythical gods and goddesses. Oh, and they also had themselves painted on the wall. How vain!

DAY 3

Another outrage! Last night, someone carved 'Aufidius was here' on my outside wall. 'Graffiti' is what humans call these attacks on walls. If Aufidius dares come back, I hope Spot the dog gets him. He's also got his picture on a big mosaic on the floor of the entrance hall (called the 'atrium'), along with 'Cave canem', which is Latin for 'Beware of the dog'.

CAVE CANEM

DAY 4

Bit scary. The nearby mountain is actually an active volcano called Vesuvius. Around lunchtime, the ground started shaking and a huge cloud of dust and ash sprouted out of Vesuvius and began raining down on Pompeii. My owners grabbed their valuables and fled. Now it's just me here under about a metre of ash and dust. Could things get any worse?

DAY 709,000 (roughly)

Yes, they could – and did. The next day, hot ash and gases engulfed and destroyed the city. Most people got away, but many also died. About 2,000 years later, archaeologists found me buried under 6 metres of ash and volcanic rock. What's left of me and the rest of the city now gives you modern-day people an insight into what ancient Roman life was like.

WHAT I LOOK LIKE TODAY

SILK-ROAD CAMEL

Hello, and welcome to a spot on the Silk Road across East Asia in about 200 CE. Excuse me if I walk and talk ...

Given the name of the route, you can probably guess what I'm carrying.

UP TO 250 KG OF SILK, DON'T YOU KNOW?

Right now, it's rush hour on the road. If you can call 5 kilometres per hour a rush. Us camels form long lines called caravans. We're loaded with goods to be traded.

PLOD!   **TRUDGE!**

Chinese silk is in demand in Rome because it is so fine and soft compared to wool.

SILK DOESN'T ITCH!

The Romans may have a massive empire, but they have no idea how silk is made. It's spun out of fibres from the cocoons of special moths.

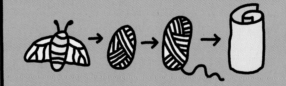

The Romans think it grows on trees.

THE IDEA IS PANTS!

CHINA KEPT THE PROCESS A SECRET FOR CENTURIES!

The Silk Road runs from China to the Mediterranean Sea.

Across hot deserts ...

THIRSTY!

... over high mountains ...

DIZZY!

... and over icy plains.

NOW I'VE REALLY GOT THE HUMP!

Luckily, I only do part of the road before my silk gets traded for stuff for me to take back. There are markets and trading posts all along the route.

The silk gets swapped for things needed in China.

GOLD AND SILVER   HORSES   IVORY

WEAPONS   WOOL   SPICES

I think I'm carrying pepper ...

ACHOO!

ROAD MAP

What we today call the Silk Road started as a trade route from China in the second century BCE. At its height, the route – actually several connecting routes – ran from China to the Mediterranean Sea, a distance of 6,400 kilometres. Camels covered most of them!

Many market towns grew up along the route, including the city of Samarkand. Boats took goods across the Mediterranean to Rome and Europe, and part of the Silk Road also extended into India.

● = A MAJOR TRADING POST

GREAT WALL OF CHINA

BEIJING

SAMARKAND

ANTIOCH

MEDITERRANEAN SEA

CHINA

GREAT ROYAL ROAD

SHANGHAI

ARABIA

INDIA

AFRICA

The Silk Road finally fell out of use in the 1400s when more goods were sent by sea instead. By this time, it had also helped to spread ideas, knowledge, religions, people and even diseases, such as the Black Death that occurred in the Middle Ages.

OOPS!

ROMAN STATUE

Welcome to Rome on 24th August, 410 CE, which, if you're interested, is a Wednesday.

 I'm a bronze statue of the Emperor Trajan, stood on a column 30 metres high.

Which is a big relief right now, given what's going on below.

The city has been invaded by the Visigoths under their king, Alaric.

Romans consider the Visigoths to be 'barbarians' – non-Romans who don't speak Latin. This label includes many opposing tribes:

 GRRR!
VISIGOTHS (FROM FRANCE)

 GRRR!
GOTHS (FROM ROMANIA)

 GRRR!
VANDALS (FROM POLAND)

 ALSO GRRR!
HUNS (FROM CENTRAL ASIA)

Citizens are calling this attack the 'Sack of Rome'.

I THOUGHT THIS WAS THE SACK OF ROME.
YES, AND THIS.

The safer city of Ravenna has now become the western Roman Empire's capital, instead of Rome.

RED = WESTERN EMPIRE
PURPLE = EASTERN EMPIRE

CONSTANTINOPLE (MODERN-DAY ISTANBUL) IS THE EASTERN EMPIRE'S CAPITAL.
RAVENNA
ROME

The Visigoths don't destroy buildings in Rome, but they do spend three days stealing valuables.

JEWELLERY
ENSLAVED PEOPLE
GOLD AND SILVER
WE'RE VERY BUSY VISIGOTHS!

Luckily, I seem to be safe up here.

SWOOP!

COO!
OI, GET OFF ME!
SPLAT!
I HATE WEDNESDAYS!

THE STATUE DISAPPEARED IN THE MIDDLE AGES, BUT THE COLUMN STILL STANDS IN ROME TODAY.

THE MIDDLE AGES

The period from the fall of the Roman Empire (476) to the arrival of Italian super-sailor Christopher Columbus in the Americas (1492) is known to historians as the Middle Ages.

It can seem like a time obsessed with faith, fighting and fantastic beasts, such as dragons and mermaids. Bloody battles were fought between followers of rival religions, empires flourished and faded, and cities and lands changed hands as they were invaded by other nations. Meanwhile, monks in monasteries were working hard to record all this history for the benefit of future generations ...

A DAY IN THE LIFE OF A ... RACEHORSE

Hello! It is 533. Welcome to the city of Constantinople. I believe you now call it Istanbul. Neigh!

Constantinople is the capital of the eastern half of the Roman Empire, known as the Byzantine Empire.

I'm part of a four-horse chariot-racing set-up called a 'quadriga'.

ERIC
DUSTY
CHARIOTEER
ME
VERA

We race on a U-shaped track called the Hippodrome in the centre of the city. It's next to the palace of the emperor, Justinian.

SEATING FOR OVER 30,000 SPECTATORS

IMPERIAL PALACE
IMPERIAL VIEWING STAND

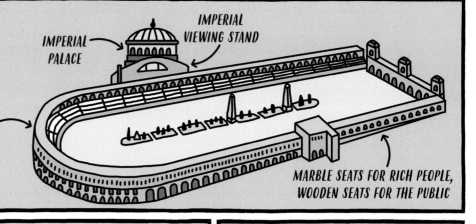

MARBLE SEATS FOR RICH PEOPLE, WOODEN SEATS FOR THE PUBLIC

Rival teams race against each other. They are called 'the Blues' and 'the Greens'.

BOO TO THE BLUES!
GRR TO THE GREENS!

The emperor supports the Blues, so the Greens shout at him.

YOU USELESS BLUE FOOL!
HOW RUDE!

And the two teams often fight outside the stadium.

I'M MEAN AND GREEN!
I'LL BEAT YOU BLACK AND BLUE!

In fact, in January 532, the Blues and Greens rioted for five days and burnt down half the city*.

OOPS ...

*KNOWN AS THE 'NIKA RIOTS'

So the emperor sent in the army and 30,000 rioters died.

IT'S A BLACK DAY FOR THE BLUES AND THE GREENS.
EEK! HELP!

Maybe one day the human race will learn some sense.

HMM ... I WOULDN'T BET ON IT!

GOLD-LEAF SHEET

Hi! I'm a sheet of thin foil known as gold leaf. I'm in an artist's workshop somewhere in Constantinople in 537.

SHINE! GLITTER!

Thanks to Emperor Justinian, I have a bright future ahead.

YOU CAN CALL ME THE KING OF BLING!

He's almost finished building a huge cathedral full of amazing artworks called the Hagia Sophia.

MY NAME MEANS 'HOLY WISDOM'.

Justinian is a Christian, so inside there are lots of religious images and artefacts, many of them bejewelled, shiny and brightly coloured.

WALL PAINTINGS

MOSAICS

BIBLES AND OTHER RELIGIOUS OBJECTS

There are also lots of small, portable religious paintings on wooden panels known as 'icons'. They are very popular.

OOH, THAT'S VERY FASHIONABLE.

YES, IT'S A FASHION ICON.

This latest style of art is called 'Byzantine' – after the empire – and I can't wait to be part of it! I wonder where I'll end up ...

Here I am! On a tile in this mosaic inside the dome of the Hagia Sophia.

Of course, the only reason the church needed building was because the old one burnt down during those stupid riots* ...

*SEE OPPOSITE.

The Hagia Sophia became a mosque when Constantinople fell to the Ottoman Empire in 1453 and four towers were added – but I'm still here!

NAZCA CONDOR

Hi! I'm an Andean condor. Welcome to what you call the Nazca Valley in Peru, in around 400.

The humans who live here meet up often at some mud mounds that they have built.

They also like to collect human heads.

WHERE DID YOU FIND THAT HEAD ON A ROPE?

IT WAS JUST HANGING AROUND ...

The site, known as Cahuachi, probably has religious importance. The Nazca people create all sorts of stuff here.

LOVELY POTTERY

AMAZING PATTERNED FABRICS AND TEXTILES

MANY HEADS

UNUSUAL SEATED BURIALS

These humans are also leaving their mark on the desert ... literally! Look at all these lines. They're made by scraping away darker stones from the surface.

SPIDER

LIZARD

HUMMINGBIRD

LONG, STRAIGHT LINE (WORK IN PROGRESS)

Some are the size of a sports field and only visible from the air.

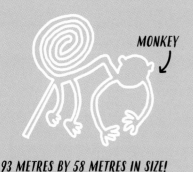
MONKEY

93 METRES BY 58 METRES IN SIZE!

The Nazca people don't write, so we don't know for definite what these lines are for.

FLAP!
FLAP!

But I believe this is meant to be a condor.

PAH! NOTHING LIKE ME!

MAYA CACAO BEAN

Welcome to somewhere in the major Maya city of Calakmul around 600.

I'm a bean inside a cacao pod which has been picked from a tree. There are lots of us in here!

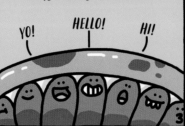

YO! HELLO! HI!

The city is one of the largest in the Maya culture, which stretches across Mexico, Belize and Guatemala. The Maya are skilled artists, builders and mathematicians.

AROUND 50,000 PEOPLE LIVE IN CALAKMUL.

THE CITY'S MAIN PYRAMID IS OVER 45 METRES HIGH.

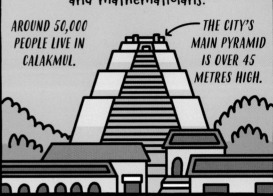

The stepped stone pyramids are giant temples.

ARE WE HALFWAY UP YET?

NO, HALFWAY DOWN!

They probably need to be so big because the Maya worship over 200 gods!

ITZAMNÁ, THE GOD OF HEAVEN, DAY AND NIGHT

CHAC, THE RAIN GOD

IXCHEL, THE MOON GODDESS

Cities are ruled by kings who have the role of communicating with the gods.

I'M A BIT FED UP WITH THE RAIN GOD RIGHT NOW!

Human sacrifices are made to keep the gods happy.

ANY VOLUNTEERS?

In return, they say the gods give them gifts, such as us cacao beans.

AH ...

Apparently, we have a part to play in making a sacred treat called 'chocolate'. Any idea what we do?

ER, WELL, YES ...

... WE GET ROASTED, GROUND UP AND MIXED WITH WATER TO MAKE A LUXURY DRINK FOR RICH PEOPLE.

YUM! FOOD OF THE GODS!

Well, that's Maya life – one day a bean, the next day a 'has-been'.

EEK! WHAT'S WRONG WITH A GLASS OF GOAT'S MILK?

ANCIENT BRITON

Hello! We're native Britons on the island you call Britain, in 600 – about 200 years after the Romans left.

GOOD RIDDANCE!

HEY! DON'T FORGET ABOUT ME!

OH NO – AN ANGLE!

A WHAT?

Angles are invaders from Anglia, (in modern-day Denmark and northern Germany). There are others, too. Since the Romans left, many tribes have invaded Britain.

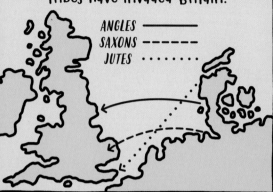

ANGLES ——
SAXONS – – – –
JUTES · · · · · ·

I'M A SAXON FROM SAXONY IN GERMANY.

AND I'M A JUTE FROM JUTLAND IN DENMARK.

YES, AND YOU'RE ALL FAR FROM WELCOME!

After the Romans left, many Britons returned to living in huts in villages rather than in cities.

NICE HOUSE!

THANKS, IT'S CALLED 'DUN-ROMAN'.

But waves of invaders drove native Britons into the west of the island.

DID YOU COME HERE IN PEACE?

NO, I CAME IN A BIG WOODEN BOAT.

Now we live in little kingdoms, often battling incoming barbarians and building defensive earthworks called dykes.

THIS SHOULD KEEP THEM OUT. UNLESS THEY'VE GOT A LADDER ...

RAISED BANK

DITCH

SHH!

HEHE!

But we also have a secret weapon on our side ...
King Arthur!

SORRY, GUYS, BUT THERE'S NO HISTORICAL EVIDENCE THAT I ACTUALLY EXISTED ...

HA!

OH NO!

NOW HOW SHALL WE DECIDE WHO OCCUPIES BRITAIN?

ERR ... TOSS FOR IT?

THIS ISN'T WHAT I MEANT ... AAAGHHH!

ANGLO-SAXONS RULED ENGLAND FOR 400 YEARS.

This masked, metal battle helmet may once have been worn by an Anglo-Saxon king. It was reconstructed from lots of tiny pieces found in a burial mound in Sutton Hoo, East Anglia, UK in 1939 and put together like a big 3D jigsaw puzzle!

A SHIP BURIAL

The mound included the remains of a ship in which the dead person had been laid.

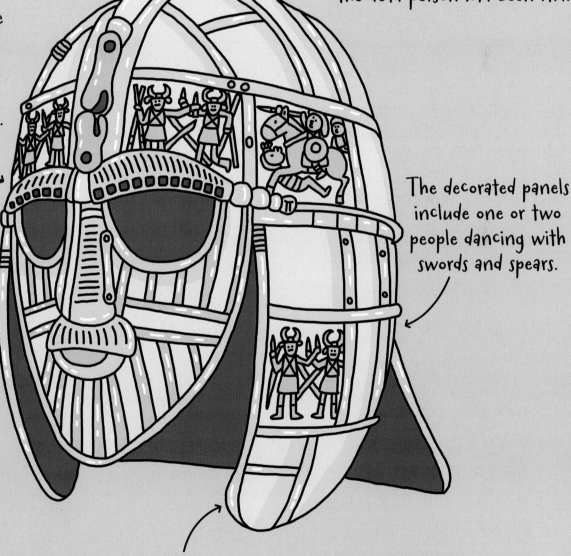

The nosepiece and eyebrows are in the form of a flying dragon.

The decorated panels include one or two people dancing with swords and spears.

The Anglo-Saxons had global contacts. Jewels on the helmet are thought to have come from as far away as Sri Lanka, and some of the silver came from Constantinople.

The secret diary of a
VIKING

An extract from the diary of Knut, a 15-year-old Norse teenager living in what is now Sweden, around 850.

ME, READY FOR A VOYAGE

SUN'S DAY (Sunday)

Big news! Today I was working on our small farm as usual when I was told I would be going on our village's next raid across the sea to England – hoping to plunder some gold and silver. This will be my first proper voyage as a 'Viking' – the name means 'raider' after all.

ME AND MUM ON OUR FARM

DAD'S MEMORIAL STONE

MOON'S DAY (Monday)

Mum is not happy about me going. My dad, Ulf Firebeard, never returned from the last raid on England, leaving her a widow. We went to visit his memorial stone this morning, which stands in a sacred place. His name is carved on it in runes, the language used by us Norse people.

My name in runes is written like this:

TYR'S DAY (Tuesday)

We have lots of gods and goddesses. Woden is king of all of them, while Tyr is the god of war, so today seemed like a good day to practise my fighting skills. My axe is nicknamed 'Skull Splitter'! Mum looked upset again and gave me a lucky charm in the shape of Thor's hammer to wear. Thor is the god who makes thunder and lightning!

WODEN'S DAY (Wednesday)

Went down to see the village preparing our longship 'Seeskimmurr' ('Sea Skimmer') for our three-day voyage, which starts tomorrow. The ship will carry 30 men, all sitting on their own treasure chests and rowing hard. Maybe it was the big dragon head at the front, but I felt excited and a little scared, too.

THOR'S DAY (Thursday)

Sooo unfair! We were due to set sail when a terrible lightning storm broke out. Thor seems unhappy, so the raid has been postponed. Mum is delighted, though. Maybe there is something in her lucky charms after all!

MUM'S LUCKY CHARM

FEMALE EMPEROR

I'm Wu Zetian. It's about 700 and I'm China's first – and only – woman emperor. But be warned ...

... my spies are everywhere! I keep a constant watch on my rivals.

WE SEE YOU!

AND HEAR YOU!

Not just in the capital Luoyang, but across the whole of my kingdom!

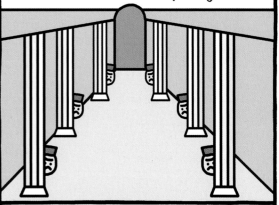

WU'S ZHOU DYNASTY LASTED FROM 690 TO 705 AND EXPANDED CHINA TO THE WEST.

I'm also prepared to get rid of anyone who stands between me and the throne – including my own sons. Isn't that right, boys?

YES, MUMMY! EEK!

EX-EMPEROR ZHONGZONG

EX-EMPEROR RUIZONG

However, on the plus side, I've reopened the Silk Road after it was closed by plague and I've put up some brilliant buildings.

GIANT WILD GOOSE PAGODA, XI'AN

ME AGAIN, FOLKS! SEE PAGES 46—47

I also promoted Buddhism by having these religious statues – known as the Longmen Grottoes sculptures – carved on cave walls.

The face of the biggest Buddha is said to be based on me!

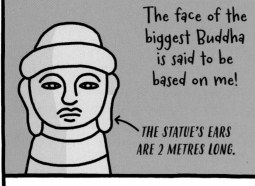

THE STATUE'S EARS ARE 2 METRES LONG.

THE VAIROCANA BUDDHA IS 17 METRES HIGH.

But, despite that, I'm not sure I'll be remembered after I'm dead and gone. Sigh! Oh well ...

I wasn't! My 6-metre-tall memorial stone has remained blank for over 1,300 years.

China was the birthplace of the 'four great inventions', some dating back over 2,000 years. All of them were revolutionary!

It was discovered that a magnetic rock called lodestone always pointed in a north-south direction when floated on a piece of wood in water. Chinese thinkers used this to create the first compass – a spoon made from lodestone resting on a bronze plate – in the third century BCE.

Gunpowder was invented in the ninth century CE. A mix of charcoal, sulfur and saltpetre was ignited to fire missiles from cannons and also to propel rockets and fireworks!

The invention of paper is credited to a court official called Cai Lun in 105 CE. He is said to have made the first sheets from a flattened mix of leaves, rags and old fishing nets.

Printing using ink on wooden blocks dates back to some time before 868 CE. We know this because this is the date on the world's oldest-known printed book, the *Diamond Sūtra*.

Other early Chinese inventions include:

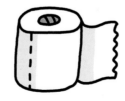

| Chopsticks (c.1200 BCE) | Porcelain (c.600 CE) | Toilet paper (c.850 CE) | Toothbrushes (c.850 CE) | Paper money (c.900 CE) |

MEDIEVAL MONK

Hello. I am Brother Michael. I'm a monk in a monastery in France around 1000.

I'm not allowed to talk to you – sorry!

I live, pray and work here, along with several hundred other monks. We have to stay silent for most of the day.

Our abbot makes sure every day follows pretty much the same routine.

MORNING
2 AM: Matins (prayers) then Bible study
5 AM: Lauds (more prayers)
6 AM: Prime (church service) then Bible study
9 AM: Terce (even more prayers) then work

AFTERNOON
Noon: Sext (sung Mass) then lunch (hooray!)
3 PM: Nones (prayers again)
4–5 PM: Vespers (guess ...)
6 PM: Compline (that's right)
Dusk: Go to bed (on a straw mattress)

My brother monks all have different jobs.

Odo makes wine ...

CHEERS!

Claude brews beer ...

CHEERS!

Hugh farms pigs.

PONG!

OH WELL, 'TIS GOD'S WORK.

I'm a scribe and my job is to copy out pages of the Bible day after day. Us monks are some of the few who can write.

It's very tiring.

Get back to work, Brother Michael.

LATER ...

ZZZZZ ...

NEWSFLASH

As different religions develop around the world, they result in some incredible architecture as well as advances in thinking and learning.

TERRIFIC TEMPLES

In 11th-century Korea, Buddhism is the dominant faith and monasteries are temples not just of religion but also of wealth and learning. Shortly afterwards, followers of the Hindu faith start to build a giant temple in the Khmer capital city of Angkor Wat. This will become the world's largest-ever religious building.

ANGKOR WAT IN MODERN-DAY CAMBODIA

ROBOT MAKER, AL-JAZARI

SMART THINKERS

Meanwhile, across many countries of the Middle East, Islam is the rising religion. Muslim scholars make many advances in science and mathematics, building on the work of the ancient Greeks, and giving us terms such as 'alchemy' and 'algebra'.

KINGS AND CONQUERORS

In England in 1066, a Saxon king called Harold is beaten in battle. His conqueror, William of Normandy, starts a royal line which claims their right to rule has been granted by God. Some 150 years later, this belief leads to a big humiliation for another English king, John, but produces one of history's most famous texts – the Magna Carta.

ENGLAND'S LAST ANGLO-SAXON KING, HAROLD II

TWO BRONZE BOWLS

A DAY IN THE LIFE OF ...

Hello. It's about 1010. I'm a bronze bowl.

AND I'M ANOTHER!

We're in a sack being carried by this Buddhist monk in Goryeo – the place you know as Korea.

CLUNK! CLUNK! CLUNK!

OOF! CAREFUL!

For some reason, we've been donated to his temple by some local villagers.

MAIN HALL

STONE PAGODA

BELL PAVILION

GRAVEL GARDEN

The arts in Goryeo are flourishing right now!

CELADON POTTERY VASE WITH CRANES AND CLOUDS

LOTUS-BLOSSOM BOWL

CAST-IRON BUDDHA HEAD

BRONZE DRAGON BUST (SCARY!)

Many objects are decorated with Buddhist emblems.

Woodblock printing is being used to produce Buddhist texts called 'Tripitakas'.

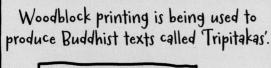

와 르
묵 슈
서 얏

All of which the king hopes will get the Buddha on his side against Goryeo's enemies.

EVERY LITTLE HELPS ...

We're hoping to play our part, too!

I WONDER WHY THEY WANT US?

MORE BRONZE FOR YOU TO MELT DOWN, O MASTER BELL MAKER.

MANY THANKS!

EEEKK!

MONTHS LATER ...

DONG!

GIANT BRONZE BELLS WERE MADE TO CALL MONKS TO PRAYER.

I'VE GOT A TERRIBLE HEADACHE.

SORRY! I CAN'T HEAR A WORD YOU'RE SAYING.

DONG!

SANDSTONE BLOCK

Angkor is the capital of the Khmer Empire in what you now call Cambodia. The temple itself is quite something to be seen.

Hello! It's about 1130 and I'm a sandstone block waiting to be carved in the temple city of Angkor Wat.

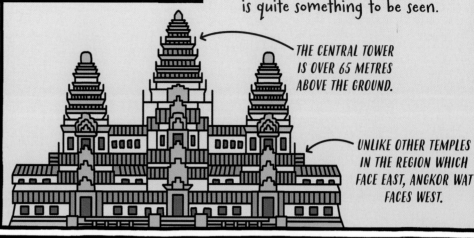

THE CENTRAL TOWER IS OVER 65 METRES ABOVE THE GROUND.

UNLIKE OTHER TEMPLES IN THE REGION WHICH FACE EAST, ANGKOR WAT FACES WEST.

It is being built by Khmer king Suryavarman II. Well, actually, by about 300,000 labourers and 6,000 elephants.

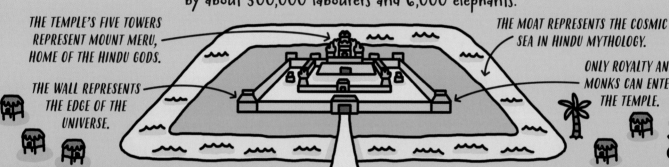

THE TEMPLE'S FIVE TOWERS REPRESENT MOUNT MERU, HOME OF THE HINDU GODS.

THE WALL REPRESENTS THE EDGE OF THE UNIVERSE.

THE MOAT REPRESENTS THE COSMIC SEA IN HINDU MYTHOLOGY.

ONLY ROYALTY AND MONKS CAN ENTER THE TEMPLE.

Not that I'll ever get to meet the king, of course – he's like a god – and neither will most ordinary citizens.

They live in the outskirts of the city in simple thatched houses. The houses are built on stilts to raise them above the summer monsoon floods.

THINK THIS RAIN WILL LAST LONG?

ONLY ABOUT THREE OR FOUR MONTHS!

Still, maybe I'll end up as part of a statue of Vishnu.

THE TEMPLE WAS POSSIBLY DEDICATED TO VISHNU, THE HINDU GOD OF PROTECTION.

Ooh! Looks like I'm about to find out.

TAP! CHIP! HIT!

LATER ...

HEY! I AM THE KING!

ANGKOR WAT CONTAINS ONE OF THE FEW SURVIVING STONE IMAGES OF SURYAVARMAN II.

The secret diary of a BAYEUX TAPESTRY MAKER

An extract from the diary of Edith, an Anglo-Saxon embroiderer, in England around 1070.

ME!

DAY 1

Big news at our embroidery workshop just outside Canterbury Cathedral today! Mistress Mabel, our manager, says we are to work on panels for a giant wall hanging. It will show the invasion of England by our new Norman overlords and their king, William, in October 1066. As I am still upset that our king, Harold (my hero!), was slain, I hid my true feelings by pretending to prick my finger on a needle.

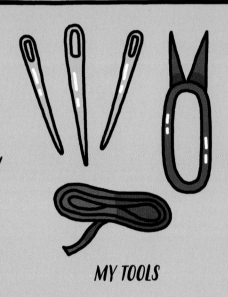

MY TOOLS

ODIOUS ODO

DAY 178

Another day spent sewing yet another linen panel. Apparently, the finished work will be almost 70 metres long! In the afternoon, we were visited by Bishop Odo of Bayeux in Normandy, who is the king's half-brother and features several times in the panels. Odo suggested he might hang the finished 'tapestry' in his cathedral in France. Fool! It isn't a tapestry – it's an embroidery.

DAY 206

Spent the morning embroidering this fiery-tailed star that appeared over England in 1066. People said it was a sign of bad luck ahead for Harold (my hero!). Sadly, they were right – and it was bad luck for me, too. I pricked my fingers five times while sewing it!

DAY 387

We're working on the battle scenes now, when William's Norman knights on horseback clashed with Harold's forces on foot on Senlac Hill in Hastings. At one point, it looked like Harold (my hero!) might win as William's knights thought their leader had been killed. But William lifted up his helmet to show his face to his troops and they rallied again (sadly). I tried to get Mary, who was sewing William, to make him look ugly but she was too scared. Probably sensible.

WILLIAM RALLIES HIS TROOPS

DAY 453

Work is finally coming to an end on the hanging. Because Harold was my hero (did I mention that?), I got to embroider his final moments. It isn't clear from the design whether he dies from an arrow in his eye or from a sword blow. Either way, he's still my hero!

HAROLD FOREVER!

ROBOT MAKER

Hello. It's about 1205 and my name is Badi al-Zaman Abu al-Izz Ismail ibn al-Razzaz al-Jazari.

I'm an inventor, and time means a lot to me.

SIMPLE CANDLE CLOCK

In fact, I've even built my own time machine!

I CREATE DETAILED DRAWINGS OF ALL MY INVENTIONS.

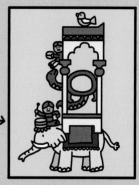

AL-JAZARI WAS THE CHIEF ENGINEER AT THE PALACE IN ARTUKLU – NOW MODERN TURKEY.

It's actually a clock in the shape of an elephant.

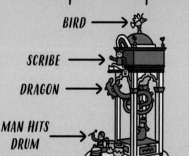

BIRD →
SCRIBE →
DRAGON →
MAN HITS DRUM →

The clock is operated by water draining away inside. Listen! It's about to strike the hour!

TWEET!

CRASH!

Time is very important in the religion of Islam. It's so we know when to pray.

IT'S TIME TO PRAY!

BETTER GET TO THE MOSQUE.

I've also found the time (geddit?) to make lots of other machines. I'm particularly well known in your day for my early robots, known as 'automatons'.

GIANT CASTLE-SHAPED CLOCK WITH 'ROBOT' MUSICIANS

'ROBOT' WAITRESS THAT SERVES WATER AND ICED TEA

WATER PUMP POWERED BY ROBOTIC COW

I COULD DO WITH A DRINK MYSELF ...

I'm writing about all my inventions in my snappily titled book, *The Book of Knowledge of Ingenious Mechanical Devices.*

PUBLISHED IN 1206

It describes 50 different devices, including the first known suction pump.

I SUCKED! BUT IN A GOOD WAY.

TWEET!

CRASH!

TIME FOR TEA, SIR?

THANKS! DON'T MIND IF I DO.

DEAD SHEEP

Baa! I'm an English sheep in a field around 1215. I love eating grass, but next time you see me I'll look very different.

CHOMP!

Told you! My skin has been made into parchment – a thin material used for writing on.

And I'm one of the most important pieces of parchment ever – I'm a document called the 'Magna Carta' ('Great Charter'), a pioneering outline of some basic human freedoms.

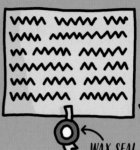

OVER 3,000 WORDS HAND-INKED IN LATIN. ONLY FOUR COPIES STILL SURVIVE.

WAX SEAL

I only exist because of this hanger-on down here ...

THE GREAT ROYAL SEAL OF KING JOHN OF ENGLAND, WHO RULED FROM 1199 TO 1216.

John – aka 'Bad King John' – was a bad king, mainly because he kept losing things.

He lost lots of land abroad ...

OOPS, CLUMSY ME!

He lost control of the country to the Pope ...

MY BAD!

And he often lost his temper.

I'M KING! JUST DO AS I SAY!

Most significantly, John lost the support of the rich English barons, who had to pay for his mistakes.

WHAT? YOU WANT MORE MONEY?

I'M KING! JUST DO AS I SAY!

In the end, 25 rebel barons raised an army and made the king agree to a set of legal rules drawn up by them.

DO IT!

STAMP!

MY FATE IS SEALED.

THE MAGNA CARTA WAS SEALED – NOT SIGNED – BY JOHN AT RUNNYMEDE MEADOW ON 15TH JUNE, 1215.

The Magna Carta said that no king was above the law and that ...

No free man shall be seized or imprisoned, or stripped of his rights or possessions [...] except by the lawful judgment of his equals or by the law of the land.

THIS CLAUSE REMAINS AN IMPORTANT LEGAL PRINCIPLE TODAY.

Of course, John went back on his word and the barons fought him yet again, until he died in October, 1216.

BAH! NOW I'VE LOST MY LIFE, TOO.

But the Magna Carta survived.

I STILL MISS EATING GRASS, THOUGH. BAA!

 A DAY IN THE LIFE OF A ...

MONGOL EMPEROR

Be afraid! It is 1225 and I am Genghis Khan, great conqueror and founder of the Mongol Empire!

Being all-powerful, I have decreed that no one can make an image of me.

And I have a gigantic empire! It includes your modern-day Mongolia, China, Iran, Iraq, parts of Russia and many other countries. At its peak, it will cover 23 million square kilometres, making it the largest unbroken land empire in the history of the world.

Legend has it that I was born in 1162 clutching a blood clot in my fist.

BOY OR GIRL?

FUTURE WARLORD, I'M AFRAID.

My father was chief of a tribe of nomadic (wandering) people who were always fighting other tribes.

GO HOME!

CAN'T, HAVEN'T GOT ONE!

But when I grew up, I hit upon a clever way to bring peace – I beat them all in battle!

By 1206, I had united all the tribes into a vast Mongol army, and I got a special title.

GENGHIS KHAN!

IT MEANS 'UNIVERSAL RULER'.

HMM ... I LIKE IT!

After that, I set about conquering other nations, destroying towns, killing and enslaving people.

ARE YOU SURE ABOUT ALL THIS DESTRUCTION, SIRE?

CAN'T YOU SEE ME SMILING?

On the plus side, I was tolerant of other religions, I banned torture and fathered thousands of children.

HE HAS MY EYES!

ER ... INDEED!

8% OF CENTRAL ASIAN MEN ARE DIRECTLY RELATED TO GENGHIS KHAN.

And when I die, I'm going to be buried in an unmarked, secret grave, not some stupid temple.

LUCKY YOU!

KHAN DIED IN 1227, POSSIBLY AFTER FALLING OFF A HORSE.

The first portrait of Genghis Khan was painted 50 years later ...

HEY, I HAD GREEN EYES!*

*POSSIBLY ...

MĀORI SETTLER

Kia ora! That's 'hi' in Māori!

Welcome to Aotearoa – what you now call New Zealand – around 1300.

Aotearoa means 'Land of the Long White Cloud'. We came far across the ocean to settle here.

MĀORI WAKA CANOE

CAN'T WE FIND A LAND OF SUNSHINE INSTEAD?!

NEW ZEALAND WAS ONE OF THE LAST TERRITORIES SETTLED BY HUMANS, AFTER SPREADING OUT ACROSS POLYNESIA.

One day, we will be known as 'Māori' – one of our words which means 'normal' people (not gods).

WE'RE NOT CLAIMING TO BE GOD-LIKE, YOU SEE.

SPEAK FOR YOURSELF!

To be fair, we have plenty of gods already – we have over 70 deities!

RANGINUI: SKY FATHER

PAPATUANUKU: EARTH MOTHER

TŪMATAUENGA: WAR GOD AND FOUNDER OF HUMANKIND

And we carve statues of our ancestors called 'tikis'.

HE'S DEFINITELY FROM YOUR SIDE OF THE FAMILY.

We place them around the small villages where we live, hunt and fish. Oh, and we brought some old friends along, too!

RATS

DOGS

HELLO AGAIN!

SWEET POTATOES AND YAMS

One of our favourite things to hunt is a 3-metre-tall bird called a giant moa.

I'M NOT GIANT – I'M JUST BIG-BONED!

Despite its size, it's easy to catch as it can't fly.

WHAT? NOW YOU TELL ME ...

YUM!

Perhaps too easy ...

HUNGRY. NO MOA?

NO MOA, NO MORE, SORRY!

THE MOA WAS HUNTED TO EXTINCTION BY SETTLERS.

ALBATROSS

Hey! I'm an albatross – one of the bird world's long-distance fliers. It's about 1320. Let's check out that tiny island.

It's called Rapa Nui – you might know it as Easter Island. It's a Polynesian island 1,900 kilometres from anywhere.

Boy, do they have some stern-looking statues here!

GIANT FIGURES CALLED 'MOAI' CARVED FROM SOFT VOLCANIC ROCK

AVERAGE HEIGHT: 4 METRES

AVERAGE WEIGHT: 12,000 KILOGRAMS

OVER 900 MOAI WERE MADE!

The statues stand in rows on stone platforms called 'ahus', and all of them look inland. It's thought they may have represented the islanders' ancestors.

EVER GET THE FEELING YOU'RE BEING WATCHED?

Some moai have red rock 'hats' that, apparently, are meant to represent hair.

I'M A NATURAL REDHEAD!

Many are painted and have eyes made from white coral, with dark stones for pupils.

LOOKING GOOD!

The humans carve the moai inside extinct volcanoes.

ARE YOU SURE IT'S EXTINCT?

YES, THAT'S JUST MY TUMMY.

RUMBLE!!

Then, somehow, they 'walk' them from the quarries and put them in position. Your historians aren't sure how they did this!

I'M NOT TELLING!

But I'm worried that the islanders are cutting down and burning so many trees. If they carry on like this, there'll be none left.

TIMBBBBEERR!

BURN!

350 YEARS LATER ...

OOPS, ALL GONE!

WHAT DID I TELL YOU?

THERE ARE VERY FEW PLANTS AND ANIMALS LEFT ON THE ISLAND TODAY.

NEWSFLASH

The Middle Ages is a period of castles and battles, knights and fights and many unnecessary deaths.

LONG WARS

In Europe and the Middle East, there are 'holy wars' between armies representing different faiths, as well as more straightforward wars over lands and riches. One conflict between the English and the French goes on for so long that historians call it the 'Hundred Years' War'. In fact, it lasted for 116 years!

THE WALLED CITY OF GREAT ZIMBABWE

GREAT WALLS

In 14th-century southern Africa, a great walled city is being built. This amazing construction will eventually give its name to a nation: Zimbabwe.

THE BLACK DEATH

Across Europe and Asia, a plague kills hundreds of millions of people – many more died than in any war before or since. In the Americas, contact with diseases brought by European settlers is soon to do similar damage to the continent's Indigenous peoples.

HOT OFF THE PRESS

On the plus side, someone in Germany invents a way to mass-produce books. History may be very bleak at times, but at least we can now read all about it.

SAMURAI SWORD

Hey! It's around 1330. I'm a katana – a super-sharp, super-scary, shiny, steel Samurai sword.

YOU FORGOT TO MENTION ME!

Samurai are warriors who serve Japan's ruler.

ALSO KNOWN AS THE SHOGUN

Here's my owner, all ready for battle.

POWERFUL BAMBOO BOW

ELABORATE ARMOUR AND HELMET DECORATED WITH SILK

HORSE RIDING AND ARCHERY ARE MAJOR SAMURAI SKILLS.

I'm a prized weapon made by the top swordsmith 'Masamune'.

SINGLE CUTTING EDGE

TWO-HANDED HANDLE

GO AWAY, PIPSQUEAK!

MASAMUNE PUT SPECIAL CRYSTALS INTO SOME BLADES SO THEY SPARKLED LIKE STARS WHEN DRAWN.

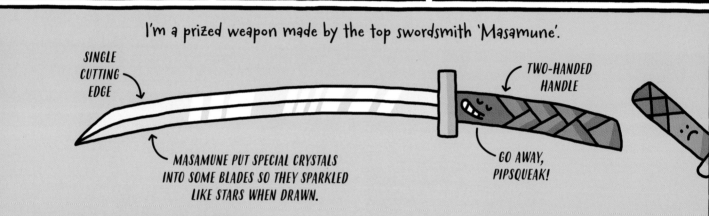

I'm over 70 centimetres long – unlike that shrimp down there.

CHARMING! I'M A 45-CENTIMETRE-LONG SWORD CALLED A WAKIZASHI.

Our owner takes us both into battles, which is considered a great honour.

HA!

PFFTH!

Along with a crazy number of other weapons ...

BO

KUSARIGAMA

NAGINATA

But, luckily, a Samurai doesn't just fight.

PRACTISES ZEN BUDDHISM

WRITES POETRY

PAINTS PICTURES

READS BOOKS

He's also trained himself to feel no pain ...

OOH, PAPER CUT – NASTY!

I FEEL NOTHING ...

A DAY IN THE LIFE OF A ...

SOAPSTONE BIRD

Hello! Welcome to southern Africa in about 1380. I'm a bird carved from a soft rock known as soapstone.

In fact, I'm taller than I look as I'm actually sat on a stone pedestal 1.5 metres high.

COO!

I'm one of many similar bird statues found along the walls of the city of Great Zimbabwe.

REAL BIRD
STONE BIRD
OI, GET OFF ME!

THE WORD 'ZIMBABWE' COMES FROM A LOCAL LANGUAGE PHRASE MEANING 'HOUSES OF STONE'.

The city was built by ancestors of the Shona people of modern Zimbabwe, who mined gold nearby.

GREAT ENCLOSURE, INCLUDING HOUSES AND WORKSHOPS

DAGA HOUSES, THATCHED WITH MUD WALLS

HILL COMPLEX WITH CAVE AND ALTAR, THOUGHT TO BE SACRED

INHABITANTS OF THE CITY

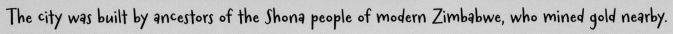

The curved walls are built from granite blocks and are over 5 metres thick in places!

LET ME IN!
EH?

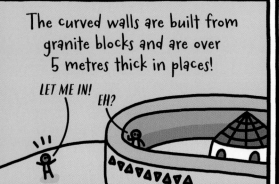

You can walk between the walls to reach a stone conical tower that is 10 metres tall.

SORRY, CAN'T HEAR YOU!

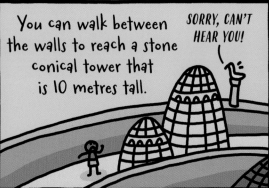

Not that I can walk or fly, being made of stone. Sigh!

Some of the thousands of people who live here travel to the coast to trade gold, copper and ivory with countries as far away as China.

MODERN-DAY CAPITAL, HARARE

GREAT ZIMBABWE

While the gold lasts, they'll stay here, I guess. And so will I. But I do envy that real bird ...

THE CITY WAS ABANDONED IN THE 15TH CENTURY.

600 YEARS LATER ...

HEY, I'M FLYING AT LAST!

ZIMBABWE PUT THE STONE BIRD ON ITS FLAG IN 1980.

AZTEC SKULL

Welcome to the Aztec city of Tenochtitlán. As you can see, I'm a human skull. I think it's about 1375. Anyone know for sure?

NO, SORRY. COMPLETELY SLIPPED MY MIND.

THE AZTECS DISPLAYED SKULLS ON RACKS CALLED 'TZOMPANTLI'.

Tenochtitlán is the capital of the whole Aztec Empire.

TENOCHTITLÁN

BY ITS END IN 1521, THE EMPIRE COVERED MOST OF CENTRAL MEXICO.

The city is built in the middle of a lake. Causeways connect it to other islands and to the shore.

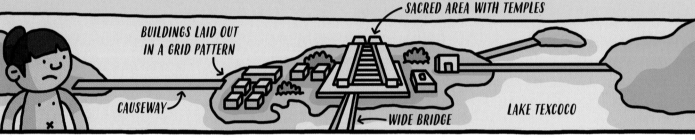

SACRED AREA WITH TEMPLES

BUILDINGS LAID OUT IN A GRID PATTERN

CAUSEWAY

WIDE BRIDGE

LAKE TEXCOCO

AT ITS PEAK, TENOCHTITLÁN WAS ONE OF THE WORLD'S LARGEST CITIES.

I used to farm maize on a floating island garden called a 'chinampa'.

OOPS! I'VE SPRUNG A LEAK!

Then, one day, I was selected to be killed to appease the sun god, Huitzilopochtli.

HAPPY TO HELP? IF IT'S THE LAST THING I DO!

On the top of a temple, my heart was held up to the gods.

I think the sun god was pleased, because he certainly came up again the next day!

THE AZTECS HAD 200 GODS – ALL REQUIRED SACRIFICES.

After that, I was cut up and bits of me were eaten by royalty.

I HOPE THEY DON'T DISAGREE WITH ME.

HOW ABOUT YOU GUYS? I WAS ENSLAVED. I WAS CAPTURED IN A BATTLE.

AH WELL. I GUESS WE ALL HAVE TO MAKE SACRIFICES. ER ...

At the centre of Tenochtitlán was a giant, stepped pyramid temple with two altars at the top. They were dedicated to Tlaloc, the rain god, and Huitzilopochtli, the sun god. It's known today as the Great Temple. It was the scene of thousands of human sacrifices.

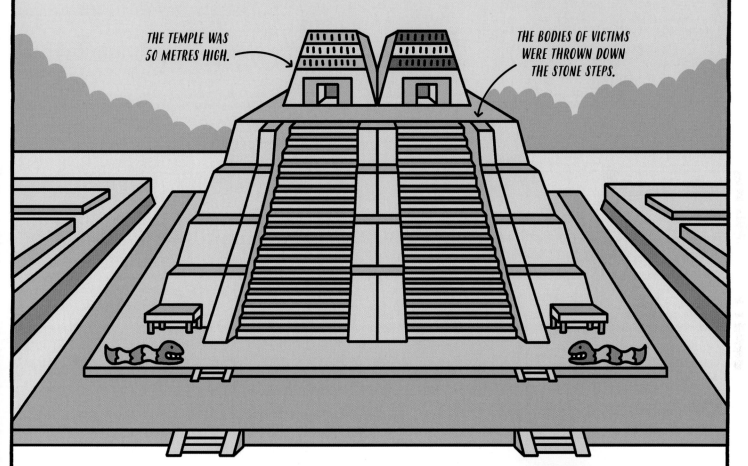

THE TEMPLE WAS 50 METRES HIGH.

THE BODIES OF VICTIMS WERE THROWN DOWN THE STONE STEPS.

The serpent statues at the base of the temple indicate that the pyramid represented Coatepec ('Serpent Mountain'), the birthplace of the sun god.

This giant carved stone known as the 'sun stone' was found in Mexico City, and would once have been part of the Great Temple. It depicts worlds from Aztec mythology.

PLAGUE CARRIER

Go away! This is Bergen in Norway in 1350 and I have the 'Great Pestilence'. Thanks to him!

YES! MY WIFE — COUGH! — BLAMES ME FOR — COUGH! — PASSING THE PLAGUE ON TO HER. COUGH!

80% OF VICTIMS DIED WITHIN EIGHT DAYS.

The disease started in Mongolia and has spread across Europe.

ORANGE = AREA AFFECTED BY 1350

← = SPREAD OF PLAGUE BY SHIPS

THE 'BLACK DEATH' – AS IT WAS LATER KNOWN – KILLED UP TO 200 MILLION PEOPLE BETWEEN 1347 AND 1351.

It causes these pus- and blood-filled swellings called buboes to appear on the neck, groin and under the armpits.

I MAY LOOK HORRID ... BUT I'M A SWELL GUY!

'Scholars' have various explanations for this plague.

A strange alignment of the planets Jupiter, Mars and Saturn on 20th March, 1345.

'Bad air' released by the action of earthquakes.

A punishment from God on the wicked.

IT'S RUDE TO POINT!

And to top it all off, I'm also being bitten alive by fleas. Cough! Shoo!

FLEA

IN CLOSE-UP ...

I CAN'T HELP BEING INCREDIBLY HUNGRY. I'M A HUMAN FLEA AND I FEED ON HUMAN BLOOD. BUT I'M NOT ALONE ...

HI! I'M A RAT FLEA!

WE FLEAS TRAVELLED OVER ON A SHIP FROM ENGLAND IN THE FUR OF A BLACK RAT LIKE THIS ONE. MY RAT DIED, SO I FEED ON HUMANS, TOO.

HI!

US RATS HAVE TRAVELLED ALL OVER EUROPE AND ASIA AT GREAT SPEED ABOARD SAILING SHIPS. THE SEA MUST BE IN OUR BLOOD!

EVEN CLOSER UP ...

THE SEA ISN'T IN HIS BLOOD — WE ARE! WE'RE A DEADLY BACTERIUM SPREAD THROUGH FLEA BITES AND BETWEEN HUMANS. AND WE CAUSED THE BLACK DEATH.

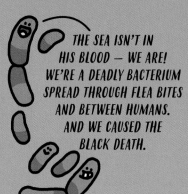

SORRY ABOUT KILLING SO MANY MILLIONS OF PEOPLE AND CHANGING THE COURSE OF HISTORY.

JUST DOING OUR DEADLY THING!

I STILL THINK IT'S YOUR FAULT!

SORRY! COUGH!

PRESS EXPRESS

Printing on paper using hand-carved wooden type was one of ancient China's great inventions (see page 59). In Europe, the slow and laborious process of producing books by hand was revolutionized in the mid-15th century by German goldsmith Johannes Gutenberg, with his invention of the mechanical printing press.

JOHANNES GUTENBERG

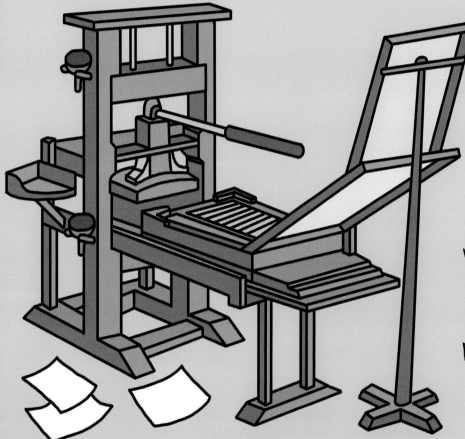

Gutenberg's press used metal type made by pouring a hot lead alloy into moulds.

Gutenberg's most famous work was a Bible printed in 1455. At the time, Bibles were mostly found in churches. Mass-produced Bibles meant people outside the Church could read the book, and debate its contents.

Europe was still recovering from the impact of the Black Death, which had caused big changes in the structure of society. Survivors had inherited money and were able to move up in the world, and buy more things, such as books.

Being able to mass-produce books made them cheaper, so more people could own and read them, spreading the ideas that helped to build the modern world. This book you're holding now is a direct result of Gutenberg's great invention!

Maps of the world looked very different in the Middle Ages to how they look now. This picture is based on a map that was made in 1457 by an unknown map maker in the Italian port of Genoa. It is as interesting for what it doesn't show as what it does.

FAMILIAR FEATURES

Although the map is an odd shape, it still has many familiar features and it's possible to identify areas of land we'd recognize today.

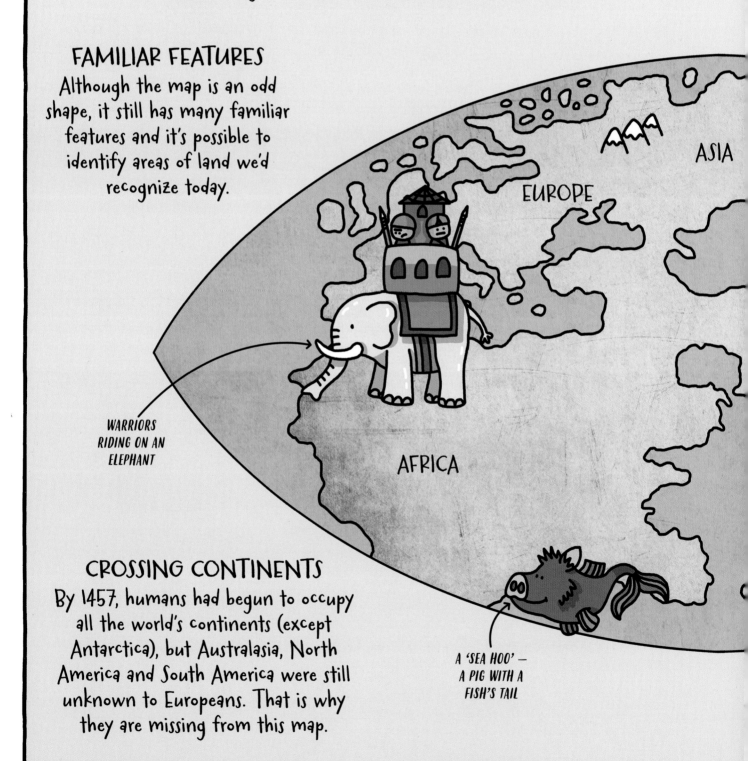

WARRIORS RIDING ON AN ELEPHANT

EUROPE

ASIA

AFRICA

A 'SEA HOO' — A PIG WITH A FISH'S TAIL

CROSSING CONTINENTS

By 1457, humans had begun to occupy all the world's continents (except Antarctica), but Australasia, North America and South America were still unknown to Europeans. That is why they are missing from this map.

MAGICAL CREATURES

As well as some surprisingly accurate depictions of mountain ranges and coastlines, it also includes some very odd mythical beasts! Some of these – such as mermaids – were simply put in by medieval map makers to fill up spaces.

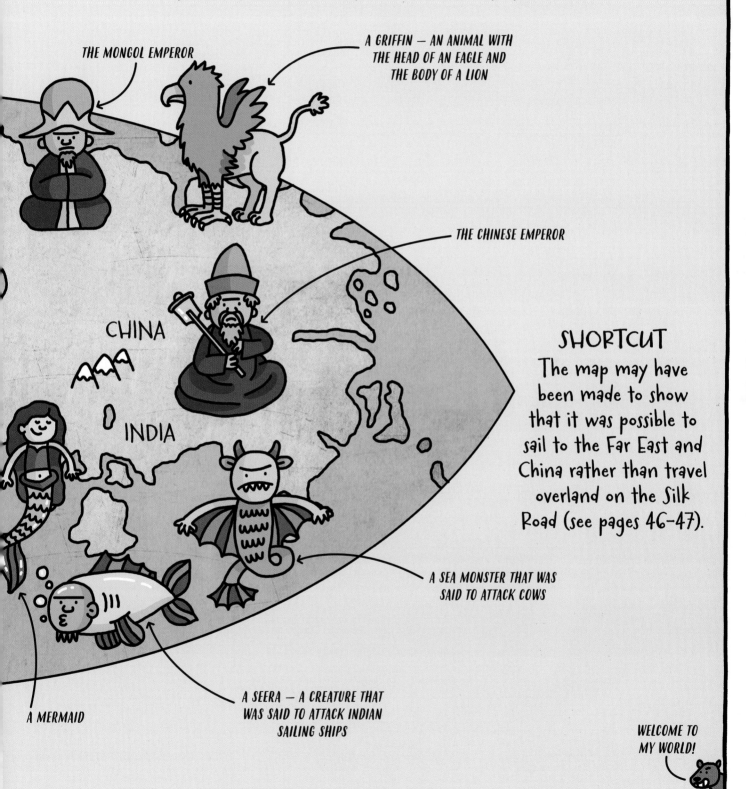

THE MONGOL EMPEROR

A GRIFFIN – AN ANIMAL WITH THE HEAD OF AN EAGLE AND THE BODY OF A LION

THE CHINESE EMPEROR

CHINA

INDIA

SHORTCUT
The map may have been made to show that it was possible to sail to the Far East and China rather than travel overland on the Silk Road (see pages 46–47).

A SEA MONSTER THAT WAS SAID TO ATTACK COWS

A SEERA – A CREATURE THAT WAS SAID TO ATTACK INDIAN SAILING SHIPS

A MERMAID

WELCOME TO MY WORLD!

GREAT NAVIGATOR

It's 1498. This is the island of Hispaniola, and I am the great navigator, Christopher Columbus.

AND I'M A PARROT.

I am on my third voyage to Asia in search of gold and spices!

WE'RE ACTUALLY IN THE AMERICAS, BUT HE WON'T ADMIT IT.

Funded by Spanish royalty, I – the Great Columbus – made my first voyage here in 1492 in search of a new route to China. The Silk Road (see page 46–47) had become very dangerous.

SPAIN

HISPANIOLA

On 12th October, 1492, on board my ship, the *Santa Maria*, I became the first European to sight this 'New World'!

HMMM ...

... *I HEARD A LOWLY LOOKOUT SPOTTED IT FIRST, BUT COLUMBUS WANTED THE GLORY AND THE HUGE REWARD MONEY ON OFFER. BESIDES, THE VIKINGS HAD LANDED IN NEWFOUNDLAND 500 YEARS EARLIER ...*

WHAT CAN WE PLUNDER HERE?

THESE GRAPES ARE GOOD!

THE VIKINGS CALLED IT 'VINE-LAND' AS IT WAS FULL OF GRAPES.

Columbus landed on an island in the Bahamas, which was already populated by friendly local people.

I invented a new term for these natives – Indians!

BECAUSE HE THOUGHT HE WAS IN INDIA, THE FOOL!

I sailed about a bit, hoping to find a shortcut to China.

IT MUST BE HERE SOMEWHERE!

No luck! So instead I sailed back to Spain with a little gold, a few plants and some people I had kidnapped.

However, on later voyages, we brought local people horses, cattle, chickens, bees and Christianity.

TRUE ...

... *AS WELL AS MANY DISEASES TO WHICH THEY HAVE NO NATURAL RESISTANCE.*

OOPS ...

TWIT!

EUROPEAN DISEASES KILLED 90% OF ALL NATIVE AMERICANS.

THE MODERN AGE

Humans have simply flown through the past 500 years – a period that historians call the Modern Age. Not only have we learned how to fly for real, we have also become increasingly speedy in everything we do – including populating and polluting the planet.

Today, we can travel, consume and communicate faster than our ancestors could ever have imagined, and we can access information in a flash. But the roots of this rush reach down through kings, queens, conquests, wars, invasions, inventions, inequality and slavery. Getting from the Middle Ages to our Modern Age required new ways of thinking, and this began with the brilliant brains of the Italian Renaissance.

The secret diary of a
WOODEN BOARD

An extract from the diary of a wooden board in the studio of painter Leonardo da Vinci, beginning around 1503.

PLAIN LITTLE ME

DAY 1

Hello! I'm just a flat panel of poplar wood – nothing special to look at. But today, Leonardo da Vinci, one of the most famous artists in the Italian city of Florence, picked ME to paint a picture on! He's quite old and very beardy, but apparently he's a genius.

OLD BEARDY

MICHELANGELO'S STATUE OF DAVID

DAY 2

I can't see now that 'Old Beardy' has started painting on me, but from what I can hear, he is painting a portrait of some rich young woman called Lisa Gherardini. While she sits for him, Old Beardy tells her about the other Italian artists he knows. One, called Michelangelo, is carving a giant stone statue of David, from the Bible story 'David and Goliath'. It's over 5 metres tall and nude. Cheeky! I hope his painting on me is properly clothed!

DAY 15

Old Beardy had lady 'Mona' Lisa back in his studio again today, but I think she is getting fed up with sitting still all the time. He hired some musicians to try to make her smile. Not sure if it worked. Maybe he should try tickling her like his paintbrushes do to me!

DAY 25

Old Beardy is still tickling me. He was telling Lisa how he bumped into some of his rival artists outside the giant cathedral in Florence today. The city is full of people with new ideas about art, architecture and science. 'O.B.' reckons it's a 'rebirth' or 'renaissance' of culture. But I wonder if the names 'Leonardo', 'Michelangelo', 'Donatello' and 'Raphael' will mean anything to anyone in the future? Certainly not to young people!

THE CATHEDRAL'S DOME

400 YEARS LATER

Sadly, Old Beardy died back in 1519. He'd moved to France but still hadn't finished my picture. Not that it seems to matter. I'm now on display in an art gallery in Paris and, apparently, I'm the world's most famous painting! No wonder 'Mona Lisa' here is smiling ... or is she?!

INCA FARMER

Hello. It's 1532 and I'm an Inca farmer.

ME TOO!

In fact, there are over 10 million of us in all.

YO! HIYA!

We live and work in 'Tahuantinsuyu' – 'Realm of the Four Parts' – our name for what is currently the biggest empire in the world.

THE INCA EMPIRE INCLUDED MODERN PERU AND PARTS OF ECUADOR, BOLIVIA, ARGENTINA, CHILE AND COLOMBIA.

Our emperor, Atahualpa, and a small group of nobles rule over us in return for taxes and 'gifts'.

MAIZE, SWEET POTATOES AND OTHER CROPS

LLAMA-WOOL FABRICS

GUINEA-PIG MEAT

POTTERY AND METALWORK

They also make us work for them for free.

THIS PLACE IS A GOLDMINE!

NOT FOR US!

But our lands are now being taken by Spanish invaders called 'conquistadors'. They started calling us all 'Inca'.

'INCA' MEANS 'RULER' IN THEIR LANGUAGE.

Our warriors only have clubs and wooden spears, while the conquistadors come with guns, swords, horses, armour and cannons. Around 7,000 Incas died in one battle, with no Spanish losses.

BOOM!

Our emperor is now a prisoner of the Spanish.

THIS IS NO WAY TO TREAT A RELATIVE OF INTI, THE SUN GOD.

And the conquistadors want to steal our gold and silver for themselves.

DON'T WORRY, WE'LL GIVE YOU SOMETHING IN RETURN.

WHAT?

ER, SMALLPOX, FLU, DIPHTHERIA AND OTHER DEADLY DISEASES YOU CAN'T FIGHT ... SORRY.

CAN WE HAVE OUR EMPEROR BACK?

MILLIONS OF INCAS DIED, AND THEIR EMPIRE ENDED IN 1572.

MAP MAKER

Hey, my name is Gerardus Mercator. The year is 1569.

And I live here!

MERCATOR'S GLOBE OF 1541

Or, if you prefer, I'm here – Duisburg (now in modern Germany).

MERCATOR'S REVOLUTIONARY MAP OF 1569

I drew and engraved this map and it made me, er, *world*-famous.

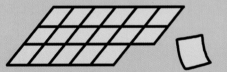

It came in 18 sheets that had to be joined together like a jigsaw.

I created my map from the most up-to-date information available.

STUFF IN BOOKS AND SEA CHARTS

ARR!

LETTERS FROM SAILORS

RAWWR! —

LEGENDS ABOUT SEA MONSTERS (OF COURSE)

I made my map for kings and aristocrats.

Most people now accept that the world is round like a ball rather than flat like a disc.

I mean it's 1569, for goodness' sake!

The problem for map makers like me is showing a round surface on a flat one. It's a bit like squashing an orange peel.

The method is called a 'projection'.

I solved the problem using clever maths – and sailors loved it!

ACCORDING TO THIS MAP, WE JUST SAIL IN A STRAIGHT LINE. ARR!

However, my projection makes landmasses further from the equator look too big.

HA! I'M BIG!

NOT FAIR!

GREENLAND

AFRICA

Greenland is much smaller than it appears on a map.

Using the same method, a human would look very odd.

THIS IS CRAZY – I'LL NEVER GET SHOES THIS SIZE!

GOOGLE MAPS STILL USES MERCATOR'S PROJECTION TODAY!

QUEEN

What do you want? It's 1588 and I am Elizabeth, Queen of England, Ireland and Wales. Show me some respect!

Hmmph!

OK, that's enough.

I am rich, powerful and a bit of a poser. I like having my portrait painted as a symbol of my power.

JEWELS

NERVOUS ARTIST

DRESS MADE FROM SILK

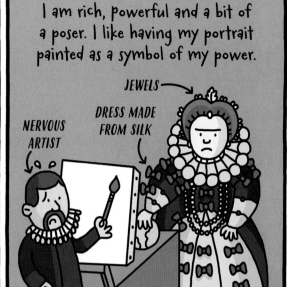

I am also very lucky. Earlier this year, bad weather helped to stop an invasion by the Spanish and their fleet of ships, known as the Armada.

WE'RE SUNK!

ENGLISH FIRE SHIP

The Spanish are cross because I'm a Protestant, not a Catholic, and I've also refused to marry their king, Philip II.

I DO?

I DON'T!

I came to the throne in 1558 after my half-sister, Mary, died. She was a Catholic queen and executed lots of Protestants.

Since then, I've executed lots of Catholics, as well as traitors and people who just annoyed me.

WELL?

YOU'RE THE BEST, HONEST! GULP!

Then again, my dad, Henry VIII, even executed my mum, Anne Boleyn!

Oh, and I'm also a really good speaker. In fact, I made a great speech to rally my troops at the time of the Armada.

I HAVE THE HEART AND STOMACH OF A KING, AND OF A KING OF ENGLAND, TOO!

HOORAY!

WELL SAID, MA'AM!

I just wish I had a few more teeth!

VERY BAD BREATH!

ELIZABETH LOVED SUGAR AND HATED DENTISTS.

Gotta go! It takes several hours to get out of this dress. Bye!

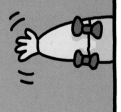

PLAY TIME

The reign of Queen Elizabeth I coincided with a golden age of European arts, including the poems and plays of William Shakespeare. Theatre-going was hugely popular, and one of the most famous theatres of the day was the Globe in London. This cutaway picture shows the structure of the Globe:

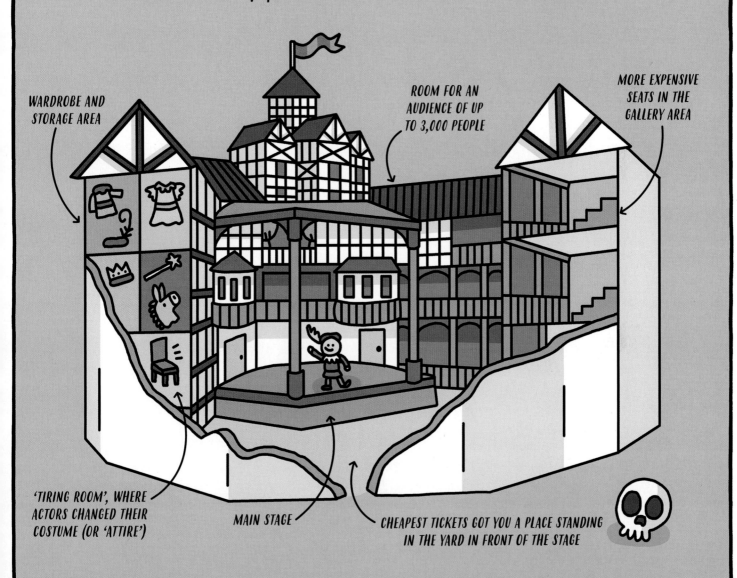

WARDROBE AND STORAGE AREA

ROOM FOR AN AUDIENCE OF UP TO 3,000 PEOPLE

MORE EXPENSIVE SEATS IN THE GALLERY AREA

'TIRING ROOM', WHERE ACTORS CHANGED THEIR COSTUME (OR 'ATTIRE')

MAIN STAGE

CHEAPEST TICKETS GOT YOU A PLACE STANDING IN THE YARD IN FRONT OF THE STAGE

Elizabethan audiences would have enjoyed snacks at the theatre, just as modern audiences do today. Popular theatre food included hazelnuts, pies and shellfish.

The Globe burned down in 1613 – it was believed to have been set on fire by an on-stage cannon. No one was hurt, but one man used ale to put out his burning breeches.

MUGHAL ARTIST

It's 1593. Welcome to Lahore, capital of the Mughal Empire in what you call Pakistan.

I'm a miniature painter called Mukund. See how tiny I am?

COCONUT

Just my 'little' joke! Actually, I create small watercolour paintings called 'miniatures'.

BRIGHT COLOURS

GOLD LEAF OFTEN ADDED

REALISTIC DEPICTIONS OF PEOPLE, PLANTS AND ANIMALS

I used 'perspective' to make myself look small. It's big in our paintings, too!

FURTHER AWAY = SMALL

CLOSER TO YOU = BIG

I'm one of 100 artists all producing miniatures for this guy ...

EMPEROR AKBAR THE GREAT (REIGNED FROM 1556 TO 1605)

Akbar and his armies have conquered much of the Indian subcontinent.

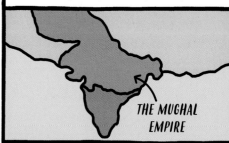

THE MUGHAL EMPIRE

Of course, you don't usually get to be called 'Great' without killing thousands of people.

OOPS ... SORRY.

THIS GESTURE WAS COMMON IN MUGHAL PAINTINGS.

Akbar has a library of over 24,000 books from many different cultures and religions.

HURRAH! WE'LL NEVER GO HUNGRY!

Even though he can't read or write himself!

OOPS AGAIN!

Despite this, us artists are illustrating a book about his colourful life.

IT'S CALLED THE *AKBARNAMA* AND HAS 114 MUGHAL PAINTINGS INSIDE.

Akbar is crazy about elephants – he owns hundreds – so there are lots in the pictures.

HE HAS A JUMBO-SIZED HERD!

WHAT DO YOU THINK?   HMMM ...

MORE ELEPHANTS!

NEWSFLASH

The early Modern Age is a period
of new horizons and discovery.

'NEW' WORLDS

After the Spanish invasion of the Americas, other
Europeans follow, some seeking a new life in the so-called
'New World'. However, the arrival of these settlers to the
Americas forever damages the lives and society of
the Indigenous people who already live there.

AMAZING DISCOVERIES

GALILEO'S TELESCOPE

Science reveals more new worlds with the invention
of the microscope and telescope – allowing humans
to see cells and stars, and prompting some big
questions about our place in the universe.

TRADING BOOM

The Dutch East India Company becomes the world's first ever
mega-corporation. It trades silks and spices brought over the seas from
India to Europe and makes some merchants very rich. However, the
company's ruthless expansion also harms the Indian population.

NEW RULES

THE TAJ MAHAL TOOK 22 YEARS TO BUILD.

In England, during the course of a civil war, King
Charles I loses his head in 1649 and the country
becomes a republic (a state not ruled by a monarch)
for 11 years. Other rulers are luckier. French king
Louis XIV builds a sparkling new palace at Versailles,
and in India, Mughal emperor Shah Jahan builds
the Taj Mahal in memory of his wife.

A DAY IN THE LIFE OF A ...

POWHATAN CHIEF

Hello! I am Opechancanough, chief of the Powhatan tribes of north-eastern America.

According to these English invaders, it's 1619. And high time they were going home!

They have set up a colony – named Jamestown, after their king – in our ancestral lands. The area is known to us as Tsenacommacah.

JAMESTOWN

PINK = POWHATAN CONFEDERACY TERRITORY

The English call our land 'Virginia' after Elizabeth I, their now deceased 'Virgin Queen'.

ME AGAIN! JUST A BIT DEAD THIS TIME.

For centuries, our people have lived here peacefully.

FARMING MAIZE AND SQUASH

SAILING DUGOUT CANOES

LIVING IN HUTS CALLED YEHAKINS

Well, we do have the occasional argument.

RIVAL TRIBES SOMETIMES FOUGHT EACH OTHER.

We also hunt tasty-looking wild animals.

BLOOMIN' HUMANS!

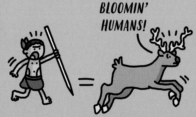

We were friendly with the English for a while ...

But now the invaders are taking more of our lands. They have also brought people from Africa against their will to work for them.

AROUND 20 CAPTIVE PEOPLE FROM ANGOLA ARRIVED IN AUGUST, 1619.

None of this is right. These are *our* lands.

AHEM, I AGREE ...

ENGLISH SETTLERS DESTROYED POWHATAN SETTLEMENTS. THEY ALSO HUNTED AMERICAN BISON TO NEAR-EXTINCTION.

The period from the early 1400s to the late 1600s saw the start of a European age of conquering and colonization. Many countries that European sailors and adventurers 'discovered' during this time were already occupied by people with their own cultures, religions and ways of life. These were often swept away as the new arrivals claimed lands in pursuit of riches, power and to expand their empires. Europeans brought new diseases and introduced destructive animals and plants. They also enslaved many of the Indigenous peoples. 'Colonies' often meant 'calamity'.

This modern map of the world shows the spread of the major European colonies by the year 1700.

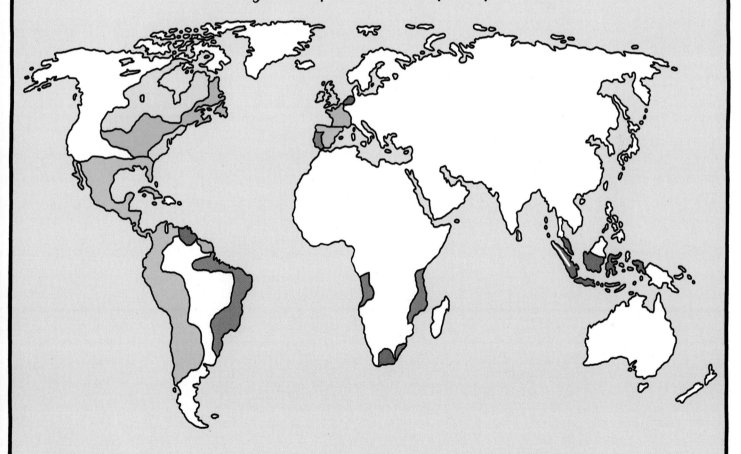

- DUTCH EMPIRE, COLONIES AND TRADING POSTS
- FRENCH EMPIRE, COLONIES AND TRADING POSTS
- SPANISH EMPIRE, COLONIES AND TRADING POSTS
- PORTUGUESE EMPIRE, COLONIES AND TRADING POSTS
- BRITISH EMPIRE, COLONIES AND TRADING POSTS

A DAY IN THE LIFE OF AN ... ASTRONOMER

Hello! It's 1634. I'm the genius Italian astronomer Galileo Galilei. So good they named me twice!

Ahem ...

SILENCE. TUMBLEWEED.

Anyway, let me show you where we are right now.

Here! On Earth ...

EARTH

MOON

MERCURY

SUN

VENUS

MARS

But don't let the Pope know I told you that.

I'm currently under house arrest in my villa outside Florence because of Pope Urban VIII, head of the Roman Catholic Church.

GALILEO SHOULD BE GRATEFUL WE DIDN'T HAVE HIM TORTURED. HE'S ONE OF THE LUCKY ONES!

Pope Urban VIII and many Christians believe Earth is the centre of the universe. This is so wrong!

This idea dates back to Aristotle.

MY BAD!

WRESTLE!

SEE PAGE 36.

I studied the skies using a brilliant new invention called the telescope. I have many home-made ones.

1.2 METRES LONG

Using my telescopes, I saw many amazing sights.

CRATERS ON THE MOON

MOONS AROUND JUPITER AND SATURN'S RINGS

ANGRY NEIGHBOURS

STOP POINTING THAT THING AT ME! GRRR!

I also showed that the Sun had spots.

OH, WELL ... EVERYBODY GETS THEM!

NEVER LOOK DIRECTLY AT THE SUN.

But all this conflicted with the Church's religious belief that the universe was perfect.

BUT YOU ARE NOT PERFECT!

So, to save my skin, I had to say that I was wrong.

MY BAD ...

HA!

GALILEO REMAINED UNDER HOUSE ARREST UNTIL HIS DEATH IN 1642.

A DAY IN THE LIFE OF A ...

TULIP

Hi! Welcome to Amsterdam, Holland, in 1637. I'm a tulip!

AHEM!

Yes, all right, we're a tulip.

— THAT'S BETTER.

← BULB

We're growing in this ornamental garden, which belongs to a wealthy Dutch merchant.

TULIPS ORIGINALLY COME FROM ASIA. THEY WERE BROUGHT TO EUROPE IN THE 1590s.

Tulips are hugely popular right now, and there are four main types ...

 COULEREN

 ROSEN

 VIOLETTEN

 BIZARDEN

The different patterns on our petals are caused by a plant virus.

Us Bizarden types are the most valuable tulips.

PFFH! SO YOU SAY ...

In fact, until recently, those crazy humans were paying amazing amounts for just a single bulb of me. And demand was so great that prices skyrocketed!

 ONE 'VICEROY' (A TYPE OF BIZARDEN) TULIP BULB COULD COST YOU =

 4 OXEN + 8 PIGS + 12 SHEEP + WHEAT AND RYE + SILVER CUP +

 2 BARRELS OF WINE + 4 BARRELS OF BEER + 1,500 KG OF BUTTER + 450 KG OF CHEESE + 1 BED + SUIT OF CLOTHES

'Tulip Mania', they called it. People made contracts last summer to buy bulbs in the winter.

WANNA BUY BULBS?

YES, I BLOOMING DO!

But this February, people suddenly came to their senses and prices collapsed.

WANNA BUY MY CONTRACT?

NO, I BLOOMING DON'T!

Crazy, really. But, whatever the price, I'm still blooming beautiful.

AHEM!

Sorry, we're still blooming beautiful.

—BETTER.

93

The secret diary of a
SCIENTIST'S CAT

An extract from the diary of Spithead, a cat in the home of English scientist, Isaac Newton.

A TRUE GENIUS (ME) AND MR NEWTON

MONDAY, 14th JUNE, 1666

Today, my so-called 'master', Mr Newton, returned to Woolsthorpe Manor, his country home. He's a hotshot scientist who usually works at a university in a city called Cambridge, but it has closed due to fears about the plague that has killed so many people in London. Well, we have a plague here, too – mice!

OUR PLAGUE

FRIDAY, 18th JUNE, 1666

Mr Newton has been in his study all week, working hard on a new form of mathematics that he calls 'calculus'. I brought him a dead mouse and he used his new maths to draw a picture showing me how many more mice we will have soon. I didn't understand it, so I just purred loudly.

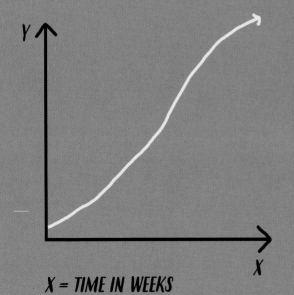

X = TIME IN WEEKS
Y = NUMBER OF MICE

THURSDAY, 8th JULY, 1666

I pushed open the door to Mr Newton's study to find him inside in complete darkness, except for a beam of bright sunlight coming through a hole in the shutters. The light fell on a funny-shaped piece of glass and split into lots of colours like a rainbow. Perhaps that's how they are made?

MR NEWTON CALLS THIS BIT OF GLASS A 'PRISM'

SATURDAY, 14th AUGUST, 1666

I now have my own little door in the study door, so I can come and go without bothering Mr Newton. Tonight, he was staring through the window at the Moon. 'I wonder what invisible force keeps it in orbit around Earth, Spithead?' he asked.

SUNDAY, 5th SEPTEMBER, 1666

Soo embarrassed! Earlier, I got stuck up an apple tree and had to be rescued by Mr Newton. As I jumped on him, I knocked an apple to the ground. He looked at it and muttered 'gravity'. Who knows what that means, but he gave me a bit of fish for supper. Result!

ME AND MR NEWTON'S BOOK

21 YEARS LATER

I'm now an old cat, but luckily I've lived to see Mr Newton hailed as a genius. He has published a book all about how 'gravity' keeps planets and comets orbiting the Sun. Oh, and three 'laws' about how objects move when you push and pull them. Well done him, I say, but if he's so smart, he can catch his own mice from now on!

NEWSFLASH

By the 1700s, people are taking the law into their own hands — whether they're pirates on the high seas or citizens overturning the monarchy in France.

PIRATES OF THE CARIBBEAN

With the sea now the world's super-highway for trade, ships are obvious targets for plunder by pirates. Many of the attacked vessels are returning to Spain with treasures looted from their American colonies. Not that the pirates plan to return it!

PETER THE GREAT

Europe's largest empire, Russia, has almost no navy — a fact which its young tsar (king), Peter the Great, is determined to change. He studies modern methods abroad, but his country is still largely one of peasant farmers, slave-like 'serfs' and old-fashioned ways.

REVOLUTION!

In France, a series of farming failures see starving people protesting on the streets to their king, Louis XVI. The bloody revolution that follows ends 1,000 years of royal rule.

AUSTRALIA

On the other side of the world, Europeans are busy invading another new continent. Early Dutch explorers call it 'New Holland', but British settlers rename it 'Australia' — regardless of what the people who already live there think.

PIRATE'S FLAG

Ahoy, there! Do you have a head for heights?

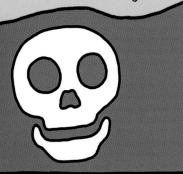

I hope so because I'm flying high on a pirate ship in 1720!

FLUTTER!

I'm a flag on a ship stolen by Captain John 'Jack' Rackham, just off the Caribbean island of Jamaica.

JAMAICA

PIRATES WERE OFTEN BRITISH SAILORS WHO ATTACKED SHIPS TAKING TREASURE FROM THE AMERICAS BACK TO EUROPE.

His nickname is Calico Jack because he likes to wear a type of cloth called calico.

ARRR! THAT I DO!

Although female pirates are rare, some of Jack's crew are women disguised as men.

ARRR!

ANNE BONNY (1698–c.1782)

ARRRRRRR!!

MARY READ (c.1695–1721)

Of course, pirates are nasty nautical thieves, but pirate crews actually have a secret code of conduct.

EQUAL VOTES ON IMPORTANT MATTERS

SET SHARES FOR DIVIDING PLUNDER

NO GAMBLING ABOARD SHIP

ANYONE WHO LOSES A LIMB GETS A PAYOUT

Plus, they'd rather scare their victims than fight them.

ARRR! THAT'S WHY I WORE FUSES IN MY HAIR!

SMOKE! SMOKE! SMOKE!

EDWARD 'BLACKBEARD' TEACH

Anyway, us 'Jolly Roger' flags only get flown just before an attack ... Wish me luck!

FLUTTER!

Ooh! They got me!

CALICO JACK WAS CAPTURED AND KILLED IN NOVEMBER, 1720.

RUSSIAN BEARD

Welcome to Russia in 1705. This is weird – I'm a beard!

TRUE, I DO!

Normally, the mouth up there gets to do all the talking.

But I've found a need to speak out, thanks to this guy ... Peter the Great, the tsar of Russia.

JUST CALL ME 'GREAT'!

'PtG' is trying to drag sleepy Russia into the modern world by creating a proper army and navy, and building a new capital.

COMING SOON: ST PETERSBURG

NAMED AFTER ME, NATURALLY!

To help him in this, he went on a tour of Europe in 1697–98.

ENGLAND   DUTCH REPUBLIC   AUSTRIA

And came back with lots of new ideas!

One of them is that Russians should dress in more up-to-date clothes ...

DARLING, THAT IS SO LAST CENTURY!

OLD STYLE

NEW STYLE

Beards are also banned for looking old-fashioned. This means the police can shave you!

SNIP!

Only the clergy and the slave-like peasant serfs are allowed to have beards.

THIS BEARD IS THE ONLY THING I OWN!

If you want to keep your beard, you can pay a tax and get a special token to show you have paid. Wealthy merchants with beards face a tax of 100 roubles a year!

ДЕНГИ ВЗАТЫ

A 'BEARD TOKEN'

Only, my owner hasn't paid his tax. It's time for me to hide!

HELLO, OFFICER!

HMMM ...

The tax ran until 1772.

PHEW! THAT WAS A CLOSE SHAVE.

BEARDIES, I'M AFTER YOU!

OR NOT, THANK GOODNESS.

KATE THE GREAT

After Peter the Great died in 1725, Russia had lots of short-lived rulers. In 1762, after a six-month reign, Emperor Peter III died, leaving his wife Catherine to rule alone as empress. In fact, Catherine was one of five female rulers to govern Russia in the 18th century, which was very unusual in the world at the time.

Catherine ruled Russia for 34 years, making her Russia's longest-serving leader. She became known as Catherine the Great, even though her actual name was Sophie and she was born in what is now Poland, not Russia.

COLOUR WAS ADDED TO THE DOMES OF ST BASIL'S CATHEDRAL IN MOSCOW DURING CATHERINE'S REIGN.

Many typically Russian things were developed in the 17th and 18th centuries that are still popular today:

TRADITIONALLY PAINTED RUSSIAN TABLEWARE, CALLED 'KHOKHLOMA'.

THE SAMOVAR — A DECORATIVE METAL CONTAINER USED TO BOIL WATER FOR TEA.

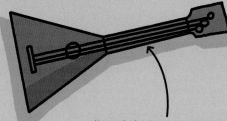

THE BALALAIKA — A GUITAR-LIKE INSTRUMENT WITH THREE STRINGS AND A TRIANGULAR BODY.

IN 1704, RUSSIA BECAME THE FIRST COUNTRY WITH A DECIMAL CURRENCY SYSTEM, COUNTING IN 10S AND 100S.

SEVERED HEAD

There's been a revolution and a big crowd of ordinary citizens are watching aristocrats get their heads cut off.

ANY LAST WORDS?

GUILLOTINE

NOT TOO MUCH OFF THE BACK, PLEASE.

Hello! Welcome to Paris in France in the year 1793. This is odd, isn't it?

I'm a severed head on a long spear called a pike – giving me a great view of what's going on!

The revolt started in 1789, when ordinary people were starving while royalty, nobles and the clergy all lived lavish lifestyles.

THE SITUATION IS REVOLTING!

AND WE ARE, TOO!

ALL PEOPLE SHOULD BE EQUAL!

YES, EQUALLY ANGRY!

On 14th July, 1789, a mob stormed the Bastille prison in Paris – a symbol of authority.

SEEMS WEIRD TO BE BREAKING INTO A PRISON ...

Later that year, a huge group of women marched up to the palace of King Louis XVI and Queen Marie-Antoinette, demanding that they sort things out.

THE PEOPLE ARE STARVING!

WERE YOU EXPECTING ANYONE, DEAR?

UGH, COMMONERS!

In the end, thousands of people were killed in the fight for equality – including the king, who was guillotined in January 1793.

BUT I'M THE HEAD OF STATE!

NOT FOR LONG!

France became a state ruled by the people, known as a republic. And soon afterwards, hated Queen Marie-Antoinette was also executed.

UGH, WHAT A PAIN IN THE NECK!

I WAS A COMMON CITIZEN. AND YOU?

I WAS A QUEEN!

WELL, WE'RE BOTH EQUAL NOW.

BAH!

SHIP'S CAT

Panel 1: Miaow! It's 1802. I'm Trim, the chief commanding officer on the British Navy ship HMS *Investigator*.

Panel 2: Though, of course, it's this human – Captain Matthew Flinders – who thinks he's in charge. (He's not.)

Panel 3: It's my job to sleep and catch mice while he sails around this giant island mapping its coast.

NEW HOLLAND

NEW SOUTH WALES — SYDNEY

FLINDERS' VOYAGE LASTED FROM JULY, 1802 TO JUNE, 1803.

Panel 4: Dutch and British invaders have named parts of it. But he wants to call it all 'Australia'.

AUSTRALIA

Panel 5: But there are people already living here, and they've been here for 50,000 years. Understandably, they aren't always pleased to see us.

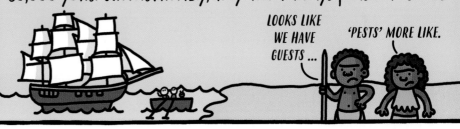

LOOKS LIKE WE HAVE GUESTS ...

'PESTS' MORE LIKE.

AUSTRALIA'S FIRST PEOPLE ARE KNOWN TODAY AS INDIGENOUS AUSTRALIANS.

Panel 6: There are over 250 different groups, each with their own language and culture that have developed over thousands of years.

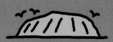

DREAMTIME – CREATION STORIES

BOOMERANG – HUNTING WEAPON

DIDGERIDOO – MUSICAL INSTRUMENT

SACRED PLACES, SUCH AS ULURU

Panel 7: Our crew includes Bungaree, an Indigenous officer who can talk to the local people.

I'LL GIVE IT A GO, CAPTAIN!

Panel 8: TALK TALK TALK

SO, BUNGAREE, ARE THEY HAPPY TO SEE US?

LET ME SUM IT UP ...

Panel 9: ... MEH!

WELL, AT LEAST THEY LIKED THE CAT.

BUNGAREE WAS THE FIRST PERSON TO BE RECORDED IN PRINT AS AN 'AUSTRALIAN'.

NEWSFLASH

It was literally 'full steam ahead' for history in the 1800s.

AGE OF STEAM

The steam engine had been invented in Britain 100 years earlier and coal-burning contraptions are powering an industrial revolution, moving workers from farms to factories, often aboard new-fangled steam locomotives.

JAPAN REOPENS

This revolution soon spreads across the world, though Japan has been in self-imposed isolation ('sakoku') for over two centuries. When this ends in 1853, Europe goes crazy for Japan's beautiful prints and decorated china.

CHARLES DARWIN

ORIGIN OF SPECIES

Science sees some big breakthroughs – the harnessing of electricity and the beginning of the battle against germs. But it is the visit of a young naturalist to some remote Pacific islands that sparks its most controversial concept: evolution.

WAR IN AMERICA

The young nation of the United States fights a war within itself that leaves over 600,000 soldiers dead. Northern 'Union' states under President Abraham Lincoln oppose southern 'Confederate' states. Southern states are largely slave-owning and the four-year-long civil war (1861–65) also becomes a battle to grant enslaved people in America their freedom.

ABRAHAM LINCOLN

FOSSIL FUEL

Welcome to Britain in 1829 – the leading industrial country in the world! Right now, I'm a lump of processed coal called 'coke'.

And I'm not alone!

The coal that I come from was formed from plants that grew over 300 million years ago – way before the dinosaurs! Like oil and gas, coal is a fossil fuel.

SEE YOU LATER!

Me and my buddies are fuel for this cutting-edge steam locomotive. It has a top speed of 48 kilometres per hour!

OPEN CARRIAGE

WATER STORE

FUEL (WE'RE HERE!)

FIREBOX

PISTON

SMOKESTACK CHIMNEY

It's called *Rocket* and it was designed by a man called Robert Stephenson.

Railways are part of Britain's 'Industrial Revolution' – replacing humans and horses with machines.

BUT I'M CUTE!

ME TOO! ARR!

For over 50 years, engineers have been building clever contraptions.

'SPINNING JENNY' FOR COTTON THREAD

'POWER LOOM' FOR WEAVING COTTON CLOTH

STEAM LOCOMOTIVE

Instead of fields and farms, lots of people now work in factories, including children. Many died young.

WHAT DO YOU HOPE TO BE WHEN YOU GROW UP?

STILL ALIVE ... COUGH!

These factories burn lots of dirty coal and coke.

SMOKIN'!

BUT THAT'S OUR JOB!

Burning fossil fuels can't harm, can it?

SEE PAGE 122.

MOUNTAIN

Hi! It's 1832 and I'm Mount Fuji, the highest peak in Japan – and also a volcano.

I'm about 115 kilometres from Japan's capital, Edo (Tokyo today), home to over 1 million people.

And just look at these pictures of me ...

Aren't I beautiful?!

They were drawn by this 71-year-old artist, Katsushika Hokusai.

I'M JUST GETTING GOOD AT THIS STUFF!

Hokusai's drawings are carved on to wooden blocks that are inked and used to create colourful prints to sell.

INITIAL DRAWING   *CARVED BLOCK*   *INK AND PAPER*   *PRINT!*

These sorts of prints – called 'ukiyo-e' – often feature actors and other ordinary people, and are usually bought by merchants.

KABUKI THEATRE ACTOR

In Edo-period Japan, merchants are considered an inferior class of people, even if they are super wealthy.

SAMURAI — *I LOOK DOWN ON THEM ALL!*

FARMERS — *I LOOK DOWN ON THEM ...*

ARTISTS AND CRAFTSPEOPLE — *I LOOK DOWN ON HIM ...*

MERCHANTS — *BAH!*

Of course, everyone has to look up to me – I'm a mountain! Even the shogun, the ruler of Japan, does.

HUMPH!

Anyway, this is Hokusai's most famous picture of me.

THE GREAT WAVE OFF KANAGAWA

Hmm, I think he could have drawn me a bit bigger ... just saying!

SORRY ...

104

A DAY IN THE LIFE OF A ...

GIANT TORTOISE

I live on one of the small islands that make up the group you humans call the Galápagos.

On a remote volcanic island, 900 kilometres from the coast of Ecuador, in October, 1835 ...

WAIT! WAIT! I'M COMING AS FAST AS I CAN.

30 MINUTES LATER ...

Phew. Hello! I'm a giant tortoise – huge but slow.

WEIGHT: 250 KG
SPEED: 60 METRES PER HOUR

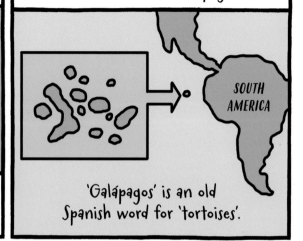

SOUTH AMERICA

'Galápagos' is an old Spanish word for 'tortoises'.

Until yesterday, there was a British ship here called HMS *Beagle*.

APPARENTLY, IT'S WIND POWERED.

ME TOO AFTER EATING TOO MUCH CACTUS!

Frankly, I'm glad to see it go. On board was this young man ...

CHARLES DARWIN'S THE NAME!

But us tortoises called him 'killer' as he was always collecting specimens.

THERE'S ANOTHER TO SEND BACK TO LONDON!

EEK!

From what I overheard, he was surprised to find that so many animals here were unique to the Galápagos.

MARINE IGUANA

VAMPIRE FINCH

GALÁPAGOS PENGUIN

And that islands had species which were quite similar but also different, like these mockingbirds.

ISLAND 1: SHORT BEAK

ISLAND 2: MEDIUM BEAK

ISLAND 3: BIG BEAK

Amazingly, other islands even have their own types of giant tortoises with different-shaped shells!

ME

COMPLETE STRANGER

DOMED SHELL (MY ISLAND)

SADDLE-BACKED SHELL (ANOTHER ISLAND)

You think *we're* slow, but it took Darwin 24 years to put forward his theory of evolution, explaining how these differences occur.

YES, AND NOW A CHAP CALLED ALFRED RUSSEL WALLACE HAS HAD THE SAME IDEA!

So Darwin got a book out sharpish!

PITY I HAVEN'T EVOLVED ENOUGH TO BE ABLE TO READ IT YET.

ON THE ORIGIN OF SPECIES

 A NIGHT IN THE LIFE OF A ...

STAR

Hello. I'm the North Star – and it's sometime in the early 1850s down on Earth.

TWINKLE!

People there use me to find their way at night ...

WE GO THAT WAY TO FREEDOM!

... including this brave woman, Harriet Tubman.

MY PARENTS CALLED ME ARAMINTA, OR 'MINTY'.

HARRIET WAS BORN INTO SLAVERY ON A PLANTATION IN MARYLAND, USA, AROUND 1820.

Even as a small girl, Harriet was treated terribly by white slave 'owners'. She had scars for life.

Maryland was just south of Pennsylvania – a state where enslaved people were free.

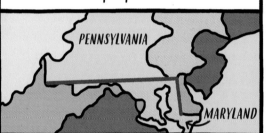

PENNSYLVANIA

MARYLAND

So, in 1849, Harriet escaped and tried to make her way there.

FOLLOW ME!

THANK GOODNESS IT ISN'T CLOUDY ...

A reward was offered for her return and slave catchers tried to find her.

Harriet travelled on the 'Underground Railroad' – a series of safe houses run by religious people and other people who fought against slavery. These secret helpers were called 'conductors'.

NIGHT 1   NIGHT 2   NIGHT 3

After reaching safety, Harriet decided to go back to help other enslaved people escape, too.

FOLLOW ME!

Over eight years, Conductor Tubman helped over 70 enslaved people through the Underground Railroad.

AND I NEVER LOST A PASSENGER.

HARRIET DIED IN 1913.

Harriet is the REAL star. No wonder the USA plans to put her on their $20 note.

106

Sadly, slavery has been common throughout history, with almost every culture and civilization guilty of it at some time – including Arab and Asian countries, as well as Europe and the Americas. For over 400 years, millions of people were stolen from their homes in Africa as part of a triangle of trade across the Atlantic Ocean.

Enslaved people were exchanged for European goods, such as weapons, cloth and metals.

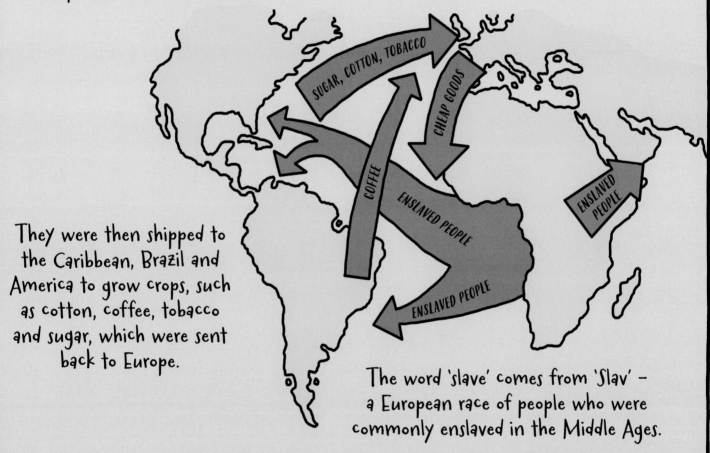

SUGAR, COTTON, TOBACCO

CHEAP GOODS

COFFEE

ENSLAVED PEOPLE

ENSLAVED PEOPLE

ENSLAVED PEOPLE

They were then shipped to the Caribbean, Brazil and America to grow crops, such as cotton, coffee, tobacco and sugar, which were sent back to Europe.

The word 'slave' comes from 'Slav' – a European race of people who were commonly enslaved in the Middle Ages.

Both America and Britain abolished the Atlantic Slave Trade in the early 19th century. However, domestic slavery continued in America and other countries for many years, and Black people faced discrimination, prejudice and violence. In the mid-20th century, Black Americans and allies began a fight for equal rights called the Civil Rights Movement (see page 119).

MICROBE

Welcome to the laboratory of French scientist Louis Pasteur in Paris in the 1860s.

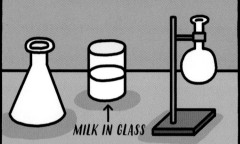

MILK IN GLASS

No, it's not the drink talking – it's a tiny microbe inside this glass of milk.

There are millions of us microbes (microscopic living things) in here. Some are capable of causing nasty diseases in you humans.

GRRR!

GRRR!

GRRR!

Until recently, people thought diseases were simply caused by 'bad air'.

YOU LOOK AWFUL!

MUST BE SOMETHING I SNIFFED.

But then busybody Pasteur wondered if tiny micro-organisms might be responsible.

IT'S JUST THE GERM OF AN IDEA, BUT HEY!

In fact, Persian scholar Ibn Sina was on to us back in 1025.

I RECKON THAT WHAT YOU CAN'T SEE CAN HURT YOU!

Then, things got worse when Dutchman Antonie van Leeuwenhoek invented the microscope in the 1670s.

I CAN SEE TINY 'ANIMALCULES' FROM INSIDE MY MOUTH!

HELP! WE'VE BEEN SPOTTED!

And now this pest Pasteur has not only proved that we exist, but also that we can be destroyed by heat!

MY EXPERIMENT INVOLVED BOILING BROTH IN SPECIAL FLASKS.

ARGH! WE REALLY ARE IN THE SOUP HERE!

His method is known as 'Pasteurization'. It involves gently warming liquids to kill us microbes off.

RATHER THAN HAVE THEM KILL US!

NOT FAIR!

Worst of all, now us 'germs' have been discovered, you'll find new ways to combat us.

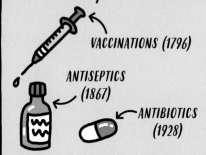

VACCINATIONS (1796)

ANTISEPTICS (1867)

ANTIBIOTICS (1928)

AH! TIME FOR MY MID-MORNING MILK ...

REVENGE IS OURS!

I'LL JUST 'PASTEURIZE' IT FIRST ...

AHHH!!

We live in a hi-tech world, but amazingly many modern machines and gadgets actually owe their origins to boffins back in the 19th century!

Electric battery
(Alessandro Volta, 1800)

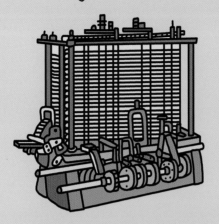

Mechanical computer
(Charles Babbage, c.1837)

Paper bag
(Margaret Knight, 1868)

Telephone (Alexander Graham Bell, 1876)

Incandescent light bulb
(Thomas Edison, 1879)

Automobile
(Karl Benz, 1885)

Dishwasher
(Josephine Cochran, 1886)

Automatic lift doors
(Alexander Miles, 1887)

Cinematograph – film camera and projector
(Lumière Brothers, 1895)

NEWSFLASH

The world is a whirlwind from 1900 onwards,
with change the only constant factor.

EQUAL RIGHTS

Slavery has been abolished in the USA and UK, but racial prejudice persists. Women are also yet to be considered the equals of men – though New Zealand will take a major step forward in 1893.

THE WORLD AT WAR

A war breaks out in Europe in 1914 that rapidly spreads across the globe. It ends in 1918 with a surrender by Germany that will lead to a second world war that begins just over two decades later.

REVOLUTION IN RUSSIA

During the First World War, the Russian royal family is overthrown and the country becomes the Communist Soviet Union. An opposing political idea, fascism, drives the rise of Nazi Germany and results in the Second World War of 1939–45.

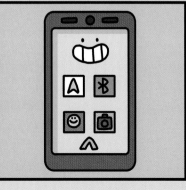

20TH- and 21ST-CENTURY TECHNOLOGY

Luckily, people have the new distractions of cinema, television, radio and recorded sound to entertain them through troubled times – all of which we can access today through a small hand-held device.

WHITE FLOWER

Hello! It's 19th September, 1893, and I'm a white flower called a camellia.

But it's this woman, Kate Sheppard, who is a budding legend!

Thanks to Kate, her adopted country of New Zealand* has become the first in the world to give women the right to vote!

WELLINGTON, WHERE PARLIAMENT IS (AND NEW ZEALAND'S MODERN-DAY CAPITAL)

*AT THE TIME, NEW ZEALAND WAS A BRITISH COLONY.

Before today, only men over 21 could vote in New Zealand's parliamentary elections.

But Kate and a group of campaigning women – called suffragists – have successfully petitioned parliament to give everyone an equal voice.

HELEN NICOL   ADA WELLS   HARRIET MORISON   AMEY DALDY

With over 30,000 signatures, their petition was so big it had to be delivered in a handcart!

JUST ONE LAST PUSH FOR WOMEN'S EQUAL – PHEW – RIGHTS!

Thanks to suffragist Meri Te Tai Mangakāhia, First Nation Māori women got the vote, too.

WELL, WE WERE HERE FIRST ...*

*SEE PAGE 69.
*SEE PAGE 69.

Male MPs in parliament wore white camellias (like me!) to show their support.

WE'RE BEST BUDS!

The anti-suffragists wore red camellias to show their opposition to women getting the vote.

MY FLOWER IS RED – AND SO IS MY FACE! GRRR!

But they lost and now the rest of the world will have to catch up!

WOMEN GETTING THE VOTE:

BRITAIN = 1918
USA = 1920
FRANCE = 1944
JAPAN = 1945
INDIA = 1947
SWITZERLAND = 1971
SAUDI ARABIA = 2015

To celebrate, Kate's now going for a bike ride wearing her 'bloomers'.

WOMEN IN TROUSERS? AN OUTRAGE!

The secret diary of a
DOG OF WAR

An extract from the diary of 'Roly', a British Army canine mascot based in the trenches in France in 1914, during the First World War.

WOOF!

22ⁿᵈ DECEMBER

Ruff! That's what it's like in our trenches here on the Western Front in France. It is icy cold, wet and muddy, and the Germans in their trenches just 30 metres in front of us kept on sending over bombs and bullets all day. Of course, my master and his fellow soldiers did the same back, while I got on with some killing myself. Today, I caught six big rats and got some tinned beef as a reward – result!

MY TALLY:

(YUM!)

OUR TRENCH

MY TALLY:

23ʳᵈ DECEMBER

Glad I'm just a small terrier and safe 2 metres below the top of our trench. My master got a break to pick the lice out of his uniform and the soldier who took his place was hit by a German sniper. Medics carried him away. Afterwards, Master cleaned his rifle in silence. I killed three more rats, but I'm not sure it cheered him up.

CHRISTMAS EVE

Someone spotted a fast-moving red object in the sky this morning and joked it was Father Christmas setting out early. Instead, it was a German war plane, so everyone took pot shots at it. My master does have an early Christmas present, though – a tin from home with sweets, sardines and biscuits in it, some of which he shared with me!

GERMAN BIPLANE

CHRISTMAS PRESENTS FROM HOME

MY TALLY:

(YUM!)

CHRISTMAS DAY

Amazingly, the day started with a singsong! Just after dawn, the Germans could be heard singing a carol, so our side sang one back. Then a German voice called out in very good English, 'Merry Christmas! Fancy a truce? A day off from fighting?' Well, to cut a long story short, soldiers from both trenches met in the 'No man's land' between them, shaking hands and swapping little gifts. Some even played football, while others shared stories about their families back home.

Despite what the generals tell us, the German soldiers seemed just like us, really. Best of all, I got tummy rubs and sausages from the German men before we all went back to our own trenches at midnight. Not so ruff!

MY TALLY:

(TRIPLE YUM!)

 A DAY IN THE LIFE OF A ...

MOVIE WRITER

Los Angeles, California, 1927 – and one young man is very worried ...

Yes. I'm so worried I'm almost lost for words – which is ironic. This is why ...

A film called *The Jazz Singer* has just been released and it's the world's first feature-length 'talking picture'.

The film is a massive hit – even though it has just two minutes of spoken dialogue – including this classic line ...

YOU AIN'T HEARD NOTHIN' YET!

He was right! Before 'talkies', so-called 'silent' movies used 'title cards' like this for dialogue:

HER: WOW, WE'RE IN A MOVIE!
HIM: I'M SPEECHLESS!

And films had live musical accompaniment.

I WISH THE PIANO PLAYER WAS SILENT – HE'S TERRIBLE!

Silent movies created some huge stars.

CHARLIE CHAPLIN
WORLD'S FIRST MEGASTAR

MARY PICKFORD
'QUEEN OF THE MOVIES'

RIN TIN TIN
DOG STAR

Though some didn't sound quite right for the talkies.

MIAOW??

CUT! YOU'RE FIRED!

MANY SILENT STARS LOST THEIR CAREERS.

Plus, the film studios made one part of Los Angeles world-famous ...

HOLLYWOODLAND

THE 'LAND' PART OF THE SIGN WAS REMOVED IN 1949.

But my job was to write the title cards – so now I need to come up with an idea myself for a smash-hit talkie ...

HMM, BUT WHAT ... ?

'DINOSAURS ESCAPE FROM A THEME PARK?' THAT'S CRAZY! YOU'RE FIRED!

THE END

FLASK OF SOUP

Hello! It's 20th May, 1932, and I'm a flask of warm chicken soup ... pretty dull, eh?

Wrong! I'm fuel for the amazing American aviator Amelia Earhart.

'AE' – as she's known – is trying to become the first woman to fly solo across the Atlantic in this bright red bird ...

LOCKHEED VEGA 5B

Back in 1922, AE became the world's highest-flying woman, reaching 4,300 metres!

IN AN OPEN-COCKPIT PLANE – BRR!

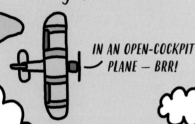

Then, in 1928, she shot to fame as the first female passenger to fly across the Atlantic.

THE TRIP TOOK 20 HOURS AND 40 MINUTES!

And in 1931 she was the first woman to fly an autogiro (a type of helicopter).

I'LL GIVE IT A SPIN!

The public are crazy about flying thanks to legends like these ...

ORVILLE AND WILBUR WRIGHT
FIRST POWERED FLIGHT (1903)

LOUIS BLÉRIOT
FIRST ENGLISH CHANNEL FLIGHT (1909)

BESSIE COLEMAN
FIRST AFRICAN-AMERICAN LICENSED PILOT (1921)

CHARLES LINDBERGH
FIRST TRANSATLANTIC SOLO FLIGHT (1927)

If AE and me can make it through these thick clouds and freezing conditions today, then she will become a legend, too.

NEED MORE SOUP! SLURP!

Exactly 14 hours, 56 minutes after take-off, we land in a field in Northern Ireland.

HAVE YOU COME FAR?

JUST FROM AMERICA!

THANKS TO MY FLASK, I BECAME THE FIRST PERSON TO FLY THE ATLANTIC TWICE!

NOW WHO SAYS SOUP ISN'T SUPER?

SADLY, AE WENT MISSING IN 1937 WHILE ATTEMPTING TO FLY AROUND THE WORLD.

LETTER 'V'

Hello. It's summer 1941 in a town in rural France and I'm a letter 'V'.

Not that this Nazi officer is pleased to see me ...

Right now, Nazi Germany, along with its fellow Axis powers, is occupying most of northern Europe.

RED = ALLIED POWERS

PURPLE = AXIS POWERS

WHITE = NEUTRAL

FRANCE, BRITAIN AND OTHER ALLIES HAD DECLARED WAR ON GERMANY BACK IN 1939 AFTER IT INVADED POLAND.

The Nazis, under their leader Adolf Hitler, are imposing their brutal military rule.

I'm a brave bit of anti-Nazi graffiti ...

ALORS!

'V' STOOD FOR 'VICTORY' AND DEFIANCE.

Other brave French citizens commit acts of sabotage and armed resistance.

WHEN THE NAZIS OCCUPIED FRANCE, FRENCH FACTORIES MAKING WEAPONS HAD TO WORK FOR THEM.

These Resistance fighters get support from military organizations in Britain.

SECRET FLIGHTS TO SMUGGLE AGENTS IN AND OUT OF FRANCE

CODED RADIO MESSAGES

REGULAR DROPS OF WEAPONS AND AMMUNITION

British boffins also provide some cleverly disguised explosives.

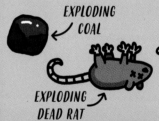

EXPLODING COAL

EXPLODING DEAD RAT

EXPLODING SOAP

However, the Nazis exact a cruel revenge for any resistance.

PEOPLE WERE KILLED AND VILLAGES WERE DESTROYED.

But they can't kill the spirit of freedom.

WE'LL NEVER SURRENDER.

I'm only written in chalk, so the Nazis can rub me out, but not what I stand for.

VICTORY IN EUROPE (VE DAY) FINALLY CAME IN MAY, 1945.

WAR AND PEACE

The First World War (1914-18) was meant to be the 'war to end all wars'. Just over 20 years later, the world was aflame again after Nazi Germany invaded Poland in 1939. The Second World War was fought between two groups of countries – the Allies and the Axis. The main Allied powers were Britain and France and, by 1941, the USA and Russia. The main Axis powers were Nazi Germany, Italy and Japan. This war would last six years and kill over 70 million people worldwide.

THE NAZIS

German dictator Adolf Hitler (who had fought in the First World War) wanted to make defeated Germany great again. Tragically, this was to be done through war, invasion, theft and mass murder.

THE ATOMIC BOMB

In August, 1945, the United States dropped atomic bombs on the Japanese cities of Hiroshima and Nagasaki. Thousands of civilians were killed and Japan surrendered – ending the war.

THE HOLOCAUST

The Nazis persecuted groups of people. These included Romanies, Slavs and Jews. Six million Jewish men, women and children were systematically murdered in concentration camps. Today, this is known as the Holocaust, or Shoah.

THE UNITED NATIONS

The United Nations, now based in New York, is an organization formed by the Allies after the Second World War in the hope of preventing such atrocities from happening again.

A DAY IN THE LIFE OF A ...

STICK OF CHALK

SQUEAK! SQUEAK! SQUEAK!

Translation: Hello! It's 1962 and I'm a piece of chalk!

SQUEAK! SQUEAK! SQUEAK!

Translation: And this is Katherine Johnson!

Katherine uses me and this chalkboard to work out the maths of the flight plans of spacecraft ... complicated stuff!

She's so clever that she's been called a 'human computer'.

BUT I DON'T NEED PLUGGING IN!

She works for the American 'NASA' space agency, and the lives of astronauts depend on her calculations being correct.

ALAN SHEPARD, FIRST AMERICAN IN SPACE IN 1961

JOHN GLENN, FIRST AMERICAN TO ORBIT EARTH IN 1962

In fact, John Glenn wouldn't launch until Katherine had given all the figures a thorough check.

AND SHE GOT IT RIGHT!

However, her life and those of her fellow African Americans weren't always considered equally valuable.

BLACK-ONLY CANTEEN	WHITE-ONLY CANTEEN

Black and white workers were kept apart, or 'segregated'.

Katherine's name was left off the research papers she worked on and she was kept out of meetings.

THIS DOESN'T COMPUTE!

But this changed in 1958 when Katherine joined NASA, which banned segregation.

In 1969, Kath's maths helped to put the first man on the Moon.

I WONDER WHEN WE'LL SEE A WOMAN UP THERE ...

IT STILL HASN'T HAPPENED.

Slavery had been abolished in America in 1865, but it didn't put an end to discrimination against Black citizens. Nearly a century later, Black Americans started a struggle for equal rights known as the Civil Rights Movement.

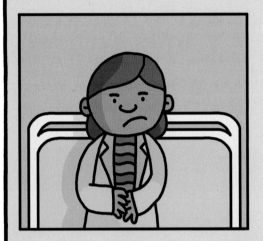

ROSA PARKS

In December 1955, a woman named Rosa Parks took a seat on a bus after a long day at work in Montgomery, Alabama. Segregation laws at the time stated that Rosa had to sit in an area at the back of the bus, which she did. When the bus driver ordered Rosa to give up her seat for a white man, she refused and was arrested. Her action ignited calls for equal rights.

MARTIN LUTHER KING, JR

Inspired by Rosa's protest, a Baptist minister called Martin Luther King, Jr co-ordinated a boycott of Montgomery's buses and led further non-violent protests calling for equal rights. In 1963, he helped to organize a peaceful march on the US capital, Washington DC. It was here that he delivered his famous 'I have a dream' speech, which became symbolic of equal rights and freedom for all people. The next year, the Civil Rights Act was signed.

All persons shall be entitled to be free, at any establishment or place, from discrimination or segregation of any kind ...

THE CIVIL RIGHTS ACT, 1964

In 1964, the US president Lyndon B. Johnson signed the Civil Rights Act, watched by Civil Rights leaders including Martin Luther King, Jr. The act banned segregation in public places and discrimination in places of work.

'SEAGULL'

Hello! Welcome to the Soviet Union in 1963. I'm a real seagull. The one you want is up there.

Yes, I'm cosmonaut Valentina Tereshkova – codename 'Chaika'*.

*'Seagull' in Russian.

For two days, 22 hours and 50 minutes, I've been orbiting at over 160 kilometres above Earth in this space capsule called Vostok 6.

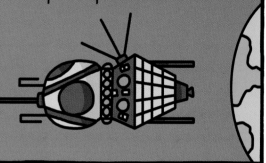

VOSTOK 6 LAUNCHED ON 16TH JUNE, 1963.

But, after 48 orbits, I'm now parachuting back to Earth, after ejecting 7 kilometres up!

ME   CAPSULE

The Soviet Union is in a 'Space Race' with the USA – and currently we seem to be winning.

SPUTNIK 1: WORLD'S FIRST SPACE SATELLITE (1957)

LAIKA: FIRST DOG TO ORBIT EARTH (1957)

YURI GAGARIN: FIRST HUMAN IN SPACE (1961)

So far, the Americans have sent lots of animals into space ...

FRUIT FLIES

MONKEYS

MICE

CHIMPS

... as well as their first astronaut.

ALAN SHEPARD IN 1961.

And they plan to land on the Moon by 1970.

THEY SUCCEEDED ON 20TH JULY, 1969. SEE PAGE 118.

But I am the first woman to fly in space! Even if the food made me sick and no one packed a toothbrush.

I also didn't tell my mum where I was going. She found out from watching TV!

HI MUM!

LITTLE VALYA?!

Now I'm down, I can't wait to get back up there!

IN 2013, AGED 76, VALENTINA VOLUNTEERED TO TAKE PART IN A FUTURE EXPEDITION TO MARS.

A DAY IN THE LIFE OF A ... SMARTPHONE

Hey! I'm a modern smartphone. Can you lend me a hand – or a finger or a thumb, at least?

THANKS!

FINGERPRINT ID WAS INTRODUCED ON PHONES IN 2004.

Just look at all my features and when they were first seen!

TOUCH-SCREEN (1992)

GPS SAT NAV (1999)

CAMERA (2000)

BLUETOOTH (2001)

WIRELESS CHARGING (2012)

I'm also incredibly compact. The very first cordless, hand-held mobile phone, developed by Motorola engineer Martin Cooper in 1973, was the size of a brick and weighed 1.1 kg!

HELP! OPERATOR! MY PHONE IS TOO HEAVY!

Crazily, early mobile phones were just used for talking.

I'M ON THE TRAIN!

WE KNOW!

Text messages (SMS) were introduced in 1992.

I'M ON THE TRAIN!

SMS STANDS FOR 'SHORT MESSAGE SERVICE'.

And what many consider to be the first smartphone came out in 1994 – the IBM 'Simon'.

20 CENTIMETRES

ONE-HOUR BATTERY LIFE – WOW!

CAN MAKE CALLS AND SEND TEXTS AND EMAILS – WOW!

However, it took until 1996 for a phone with internet access to appear.

THE NOKIA 'COMMUNICATOR'

The Web had been invented in 1989 by Tim Berners-Lee.

IT'S WWW-ONDERFUL!

Nowadays, smartphones put a world of information into the hands of over 3.5 billion people.

HMM ... I THINK I'LL JUST CHECK THAT FIGURE ...

Not that all those users are smart ...
OOPS! DROPPED IT!

HELP!

ALLEGEDLY, 19% OF PHONE DAMAGE IS CAUSED BY TOILET WATER!

Luckily, there are still other ways to find things out ...

LIBRARY

GOT ANY BOOKS ON HISTORY?

YES!

121

A DAY IN THE LIFE OF A ... CARBON ATOM

Hi! Welcome to somewhere high in the air. I'm a carbon atom.

HEY!

EXCUSE ME?!

OK. I'm actually part of a molecule of carbon dioxide (CO_2) gas along with these oxygen atoms.

HUMPH!

THAT'S BETTER.

There are literally tonnes of us in the air around Earth – and our numbers are growing all the time.

NICE PLANET!

YES, IT'S GOT A LOVELY ATMOSPHERE. WARM, THOUGH ...

That's because since the Industrial Revolution, 250 years ago, you've been burning fossil fuels such as oil, gas and coal.

— REMEMBER ME?

SEE PAGE 103.

When that coke was burned, the carbon in it was released as CO_2 gas molecules, like me.

FREE AT LAST!

IS IT ME OR IS IT HOT IN HERE?

CO_2, along with water vapour and methane, is a so-called 'greenhouse gas'.

THE SUN'S HEAT GETS TRAPPED INSIDE.

All your clever inventions have been adding CO_2 for centuries.

LIGHT AND HEAT

TRANSPORT

INDUSTRY AND BUILDING

Intensive farming also adds methane gas (CH_4) from the bums and burps of livestock.

OOPS! EXCUSE ME!

All us gases cause global warming – one of the most pressing problems facing the world today.

NOT WELL ... TOO WARM.

One which could make all you humans history, too ...

STRIKE FOR CLIMATE!

But luckily you've got lots of clever 'green' solutions. Good luck!

WIND POWER

SOLAR POWER

MORE TREES

BRILLIANT BRAINS

A DAY IN THE LIFE OF ...

THE FUTURE

Hello! I'm a fragment of the future.

History never stops happening, so who knows what I might be?

After reading this book, you've seen lots of stuff that happened in the past.

So, I could be something bad, something good or hopefully ...

... something BRILLIANT!

It might even involve YOU. So, go ahead and imagine some history that hasn't happened yet ...

Wow! Looking forward to that. Have a great day! Byeeee!

GOODBYE!

SEE YA!

THANKS FOR READING!

GLOSSARY

It turns out that there is a lot going on in a single day, as well as lots of new terms to learn. This glossary gives you a brief explanation of some of the harder words you may have come across.

Archaeologist
A person who studies objects made by humans in the past in order to learn how people lived.

Aristocrat
A person who has a high social position and who usually belongs to a wealthy and privileged family.

Automaton
Another word for a robot.

Buddhism
A religion based on the teachings of the Buddha, which began in India over 2,500 years ago.

Catholicism
The oldest branch of the Christian religion, which follows the beliefs of the Bible. The Catholic Church is led by the Pope.

Civilization
A group of people living in a large, well-established setting, such as a town or city. These people share language and culture, and have systems such as agriculture and government.

Civil Rights
The rights that a ruler or government gives to its citizens – who can vote and who can be educated, for instance. People have fought for more equal civil rights throughout history. In 1950s America, the Civil Rights Movement was a peaceful campaign that aimed to give Black Americans the same rights as white Americans.

Colony
A group of people who move from one country to another and declare that the land they have settled on belongs to their home country.

Conquistador
The Spanish word for 'conqueror', a conquistador was a Spanish or Portuguese explorer or soldier who invaded the Americas in the 1500s.

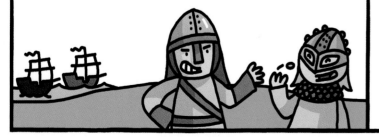

Culture
The way of life shared by a group of people – this may include language, clothing, music, art, beliefs, customs, food and religion.

Domestication
The process of taming a wild animal or plant so that it can be used by or live closely alongside humans.

Dyke
A structure, usually made up of an earth bank and ditch, often built for defence in Anglo-Saxon Britain.

Embroidery
A type of craft in which patterns or pictures are sewn on to fabric.

Empire
A group of regions and lands which are controlled by one ruler or government.

Evolution
The process through which simple life forms adapted and changed over time to create the millions of living things alive in the world today.

Extinction
The death of the last remaining member of a species.

Fascism
A political belief that the strength of the country is more important than the well-being of the people. Fascist governments use violence and rule with unlimited power. Adolf Hitler was a fascist leader.

Fossil Fuel
A fuel formed through the buried remains of ancient plants and animals. Coal, natural gas and oil are examples.

Hieroglyph
A picture or symbol used to represent a word in a writing system, such as that of ancient Egypt.

Hinduism
The world's oldest major religion, which dates back over 3,000 years. Hindus worship many gods and believe their soul will be reborn when they die.

Ice Age
A period when the temperature of the Earth's surface and atmosphere drops, and huge glaciers cover large areas of the planet. Ice ages have happened several times during Earth's history – the last ice age ended about 10,000 years ago.

Industrial Revolution
The period from the late 1700s to the mid-1800s in Europe and the USA, when people moved from the countryside to cities and changed from making things by hand to making things in factories.

Irrigation
The process of adding water to farmland to help crops grow.

Islam
One of the world's major religions, which follows the teachings of the Quran. Followers of Islam are called Muslims and their place of worship is called a mosque.

Microbe
One of many billions of tiny living things that include bacteria, algae, fungi and viruses. Most are essential to life on Earth. Also called a micro-organism.

Nomad
A person who travels from place to place rather than living in a fixed setting, such as a town.

Pilgrim
A person who travels to another country or specific place, usually for a religious reason.

Plague
A deadly disease caused by bacteria. The Black Death was a name given to an outbreak of plague in Europe and Asia in the 1300s, which caused the deaths of up to 200 million people.

Protestantism
A branch of the Christian religion, which follows the beliefs of the Bible. The first Protestant churches were set up in the 1500s by people who wanted to break away from the Catholic Church. This movement was known as the Reformation.

Renaissance
Meaning 'rebirth' in French, the Renaissance was a period in Europe between the 1300s and 1500s. It was a time of free-thinking and great developments in art and science.

Revolution
A sudden change in how things are run and who has power, usually sparked by a rebellion of the people. In the 1700s, there were major revolutions in France and America, for example.

Segregation
When people are kept apart. Usually, this means one group of people is being treated unfairly or discriminated against.

Suffrage
The right to vote. In many societies throughout history, only certain people were allowed to vote. In the early 1900s, for example, women across the world struggled for years to get the right to vote.

Tax
A sum of money paid by ordinary people to their government or ruler. Taxes are usually in place to help the government pay for something (such as schools or police) or to try to change people's behaviour (to stop eating unhealthy food, for example).

ABOUT MIKE AND JESS

What do Mike Barfield and Jess Bradley get up to all day, eh? Find out below!

Mike Barfield is a writer, cartoonist, poet and performer, who lives in a small village in North Yorkshire, England. A typical day in his life consists of sitting at a desk in a very untidy room surrounded by hundreds of books, while he writes and draws things that he hopes will make people laugh. He drinks gallons of tea while he does so.

Jess Bradley is an illustrator and comic artist from Torquay, England. As well as writing and drawing for *The Phoenix*, she also writes for *The Beano* and illustrates a variety of children's books. During her day, she enjoys painting in her sketchbooks, watching scary films and letting her son beat her at Mario Kart.